C. R. Mart.

SMP 11-16

Book B5

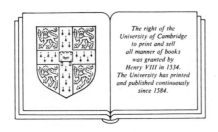

The right of the
University of Cambridge
to print and sell
all manner of books
was granted by
Henry VIII in 1534.
The University has printed
and published continuously
since 1584.

Cambridge University Press

Cambridge
New York   New Rochelle   Melbourne   Sydney

Published by the Press Syndicate of the University of Cambridge
The Pitt Building, Trumpington Street, Cambridge CB2 1RP
32 East 57th Street, New York, NY 10022, USA
10 Stamford Road, Oakleigh, Melbourne 3166, Australia

First published 1987

Illustrations by Chris Evans, Tim Howe and David Parkins
Diagrams and phototypesetting by Parkway Group, London and
Abingdon, and Gecko Limited, Bicester, Oxon.

Printed in Great Britain by Scotprint, Musselburgh, Scotland

British Library cataloguing in publication data
SMP 11–16 blue series.
Bk B5
    1. Mathematics – 1961–
    I. School Mathematics Project
    510   QA39.2
ISBN 0 521 31468 2

Acknowledgements
The authors and the publisher would like to thank the following for permission to
reproduce copyright material:
Handford Photography and Costain Civil Engineering (cover); Aerofilms Ltd (page 36);
Historic Buildings & Monuments Commission for England (pages 36, 37); Ordnance
Survey – Crown copyright reserved (pages 38, 44); *The Times* (page 65); Thomas Cook
(page 67)

Contents

1 Speed

A Distance, speed and time

If a coach travels on a motorway at a steady speed of 60 m.p.h., this means that it goes 60 miles in each hour.

So in 2 hours it will go 120 miles, in 3 hours it will go 180 miles, and so on.

We can calculate the distance travelled by multiplying the speed, 60 m.p.h., by the time in hours.

$$\text{Distance in miles} = \text{Speed in m.p.h.} \times \text{Time in hours}$$

We can also measure the speed of an object in kilometres per hour (km/h), metres per second (m/s), and so on.
If we use m/s, the formula becomes

$$\text{Distance in metres} = \text{Speed in m/s} \times \text{Time in seconds}$$

So, for example, if a model car travels at 4 m/s for 8 seconds, the distance it goes is $4 \times 8 = 32$ metres.

A1   An ambulance travels at 70 m.p.h. for 3 hours. How far does it travel in that time?

A2   A veteran car travels at 15 m.p.h. for 5 hours. How far does it travel in that time?

A3   An aircraft travels at a steady speed of 600 km/h for $4\frac{1}{2}$ hours. How far does it travel?

A4   A model speedboat travels at 2·5 m/s for 16 seconds. How far does it travel?

A5   A mole burrows through the earth at a speed of 18 cm per minute.

How far will it burrow in 15 minutes? Write the answer in **metres**.

1

The diagram below shows some speeds in m.p.h., km/h and m/s.

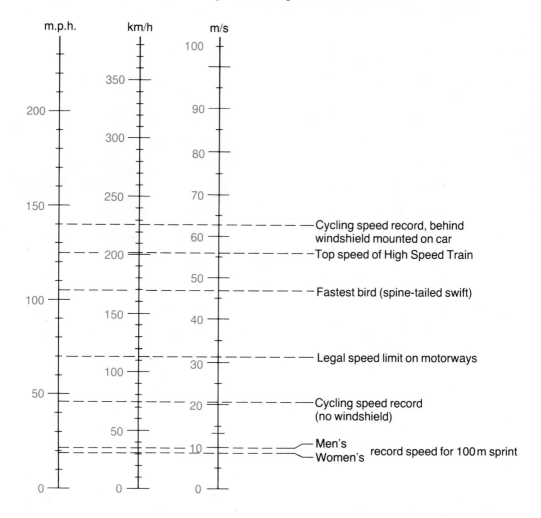

A6 Find the dotted line for the fastest bird (the spine-tailed swift). Use the scales to estimate its speed in

(a) m.p.h.   (b) km/h   (c) m/s

The scales can be used to change m.p.h. to km/h, m.p.h. to m/s, and so on. To do this you put a ruler across the scales.

A7 Put a ruler across the scales through the mark for 200 m.p.h. Use the other scales to change 200 m.p.h. to   (a) km/h   (b) m/s as accurately as you can.

A8 Judy is riding her motorbike at 30 m.p.h. Use the scales to change 30 m.p.h. to m/s, as accurately as you can, and work out how many metres Judy travels in 10 seconds.

Most moving objects do not travel at a steady, or constant, speed.
They slow up sometimes and go faster at other times.

For example, it is impossible to drive a car on a motorway at a
constant speed for more than a few minutes, unless there is no other
traffic around.

Suppose a car takes 3 hours to travel a distance of 120 miles.
We say its **average** speed is 40 m.p.h., because $\frac{120}{3} = 40$.

The car probably went faster than 40 m.p.h. sometimes, and slower than
40 m.p.h. at other times. But in 3 hours it went 120 miles, which is the
distance it would have gone if its speed had been 40 m.p.h. all the time.

To find the average speed, you divide the distance by the time.

$$\text{Average speed in m.p.h.} = \frac{\text{Distance in miles}}{\text{Time in hours}}$$

A9 Sally takes 2 hours to cycle a distance of 18 miles.
Calculate her average speed in m.p.h.

A10 Bruce takes $2\frac{1}{2}$ hours to cycle a distance of 20 miles.
Calculate his average speed in m.p.h.

A11 The distance by sea from Harwich to the Hook of Holland
is 121 miles. The crossing by ferry takes $6\frac{3}{4}$ hours.

Calculate the average speed of the ferry, to the nearest m.p.h.

Suppose one train takes 3 hours to travel 180 miles, and another
train takes 4 hours to travel 200 miles.

The first train's average speed is $\frac{180}{3} = 60$ m.p.h.

The second train's average speed is $\frac{200}{4} = 50$ m.p.h.

We say the first train is **faster on average** than the second train.

A12 (a) Calculate the average speed of each of these coaches, to
the nearest m.p.h.

(i) A coach which travels from Exeter to Manchester, a distance
of 235 miles, in $4\frac{3}{4}$ hours

(ii) A coach which takes $4\frac{1}{4}$ hours to travel from Carlisle
to Birmingham, a distance of 196 miles

(b) Which coach is faster, on average?

3

B Calculating journey times

A steam traction engine is on its way to a rally. It is being driven from Dover to Canterbury, a distance of 15 miles.

The traction engine's speed is 5 m.p.h.

In each hour it does 5 miles, so it will take **3 hours** to go 15 miles.

We work out the journey time by dividing the distance, 15 miles, by the speed, 5 m.p.h.

$$\text{Time in hours} = \frac{\text{Distance in miles}}{\text{Speed in m.p.h.}}$$

B1 Tina has a motorboat which travels at 8 m.p.h.
She plans to make a journey of 40 miles in the boat.
How long will the journey take?

B2 The ships which are used for sea crossings from Britain to Ireland, the continent, etc., travel at 18 m.p.h.

Calculate the time taken for each of these crossings, to the nearest hour.

(a) Newhaven to Dieppe, 73 miles

(b) Southampton to Le Havre, 130 miles

(c) Stranraer to Larne, 40 miles

B3 Karen has driven a lot on motorways, and she has found that in ordinary traffic conditions she can average about 50 m.p.h.

Calculate the time it would take her to drive on the motorway from Bristol to Carlisle, a distance of 477 miles. Give the time to the **nearest half-hour**.

B4 Canal boats travel at about 3 m.p.h. There are locks on canals where the water level is raised or lowered. It takes a boat about $\frac{1}{4}$ hour to go through a lock.

Here is a map of a stretch of canal. Locks are marked ⇒ and distances are in miles.

Work out the time it would take to travel from A to B.

The relationship between speed and journey time

The distance by road from Liverpool to Exeter is 240 miles.

Suppose a veteran car does the journey at a speed of 10 m.p.h.

The journey time (not counting stops) is

$$\frac{240}{10} = 24 \text{ hours}.$$

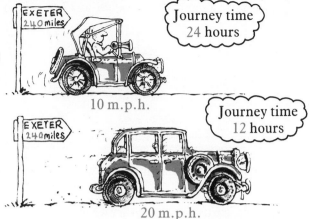

If a slightly more modern car does the journey at a speed of 20 m.p.h., the

journey time will be $\frac{240}{20} = 12$ **hours.**

B5 (a) Calculate the time taken to travel the 240 miles from Liverpool to Exeter at a speed of

   (i) 30 m.p.h.   (ii) 40 m.p.h.   (iii) 50 m.p.h.   (iv) 60 m.p.h.

   (b) Make a table like this and write your answers to part (a) in it.

Speed in m.p.h.	10	20	30	40	50	60
Journey time in hours	24	12				

   (c) Draw axes on graph paper. Use the scales shown here.

   Plot the points from your table, and draw a smooth curve through them.

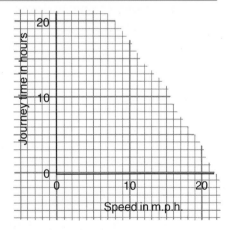

The journey time decreases if the speed increases.

Doubling the speed means halving the journey time.
For example, if we do a journey at 40 m.p.h. instead of 20 m.p.h., the journey will take only half the time.

This is obvious really, because if you go twice as far in each hour, then you will only need half the number of hours.

Also, if you go three times as far in each hour (for example, at 60 m.p.h. instead of 20 m.p.h.) then you will only need $\frac{1}{3}$ the number of hours.

5

C Decimals of an hour (1)

Suppose a boat which travels at **17 m.p.h.** has to do a journey of **58 miles**.

17 m.p.h.

58 miles

We can use the formula $\text{Time} = \dfrac{\text{Distance}}{\text{Speed}}$ to find the journey time.

When we use a calculator, we get $\dfrac{58}{17} = 3{\cdot}41$ (to 2 d.p.).

This means **3·41 hours**

not 3 hours 41 minutes.

Calculators work in decimals. So the answer 3·41 is in **decimals of an hour**.

We usually think of time in hours and minutes, so we need to be able to change decimals of an hour into minutes.

> To change hours to minutes, multiply by 60.

This is obviously true for whole numbers of hours. For example, 2 hours is $2 \times 60 = 120$ minutes. The rule is also true for decimals of an hour.

The answer we got above was 3·41 hours. That's 3 hours and 0·41 hour. So we need to change 0·41 hour into minutes.

$$0{\cdot}41 \times 60 = 24{\cdot}6 \text{ minutes}$$
$$= 25 \text{ minutes, to the nearest minute}$$

So 3·41 hours = **3 hours and 25 minutes**, to the nearest minute.

C1 Change these to hours and minutes, to the nearest minute.

(a) 2·5 hours   (b) 5·72 hours   (c) 3·03 hours   (d) 15·85 hours

C2 (a) Use a calculator to find the time taken, in hours, to travel a distance of 115 miles at a speed of 35 m.p.h. Give the answer to 2 d.p.

(b) Change the answer to (a) into hours and minutes.

C3　Find the time taken to do these journeys. Give each time in hours and minutes, to the nearest minute.

(a)　A journey of 145 miles at a speed of 55 m.p.h.

(b)　A journey of 385 miles at a speed of 125 m.p.h.

(c)　A journey of 65 miles at a speed of 90 m.p.h.

(d)　A journey of 48 miles at a speed of 110 m.p.h.

C4　A light aircraft sets out on a journey of 685 miles.

It travels at a speed of 155 m.p.h.

(a)　Calculate the journey time in hours and minutes.

(b)　If the aircraft sets out at 6:30 a.m., at what time will it finish the journey?

C5　A motor boat travels at a speed of 18 m.p.h. The boat sets out on a journey of 49 miles.

(a)　How long will the journey take, in hours and minutes?

(b)　If the boat starts out at 3:15 p.m., at what time will it finish the journey?

C6　A damaged ship is drifting at a speed of 3·5 m.p.h. towards some rocks.

At 2:45 p.m. the ship is 18·7 miles from the rocks.

(a)　How long will it take, in hours and minutes, for the ship to reach the rocks?

(b)　At what time will it reach the rocks?

C7　A steamer on a lake travels from the northern end of the lake to the southern end at a speed of 13 m.p.h.

The distance from the northern end to the southern end is 63 miles.

If the steamer leaves the northern end at 2:30 p.m., at what time will it arrive at the southern end?

Distances by sea are often measured in **nautical miles**.
A nautical mile is longer than an ordinary mile: it is about 1·15 miles.

A speed of 1 nautical mile per hour is called **1 knot**.

D Decimals of an hour (2)

A coach takes 2 hours 35 minutes to travel 118 miles.

To find the average speed, we use the formula Average speed $= \dfrac{\text{Distance}}{\text{Time}}$.

> The time has to be in **hours**, if we want the speed to be in m.p.h.

> So we have to change the minutes in '2 hours 35 minutes' to a decimal of an hour. The rule for this is:
>
> To change minutes to hours, divide by 60.

So 35 minutes $= \dfrac{35}{60} = 0 \cdot 58$ hour, to 2 d.p.

So 2 hours 35 minutes becomes **2·58 hours**.

Now we can use the formula.

$$\text{Average speed} = \frac{\text{Distance}}{\text{Time}} = \frac{118}{2 \cdot 58} = \textbf{46 m.p.h.} \text{ (to the nearest 1 m.p.h.)}$$

D1 Change these to hours, to 2 decimal places.

(a) 4 hours 16 minutes   (b) 3 hours 7 minutes

(c) 8 hours 50 minutes   (d) 4 hours 47 minutes

(e) 13 minutes   (f) 28 minutes   (g) 51 minutes

D2 A train travels a distance of 64 miles in 1 hour 23 minutes.

Calculate the train's average speed, to the nearest 1 m.p.h.

D3 Calculate the average speed of each of these, to the nearest 1 m.p.h.

(a) A car which travels 72 miles in 1 hour 42 minutes

(b) A bicycle which travels 19 miles in 2 hours 9 minutes

(c) An athlete who runs 23 miles in 3 hours 37 minutes

D4 A coach leaves London at 5:15 p.m. and arrives at Bristol at 7:50 p.m. The distance from London to Bristol is 119 miles.

(a) How long does the coach take to travel from London to Bristol, in hours and minutes?

(b) Calculate the average speed of the coach, to the nearest 1 m.p.h.

8

E Mixed questions

Sometimes in these questions you have to calculate a **speed**, sometimes a **distance** and sometimes a **time**.

E1 A and B are two aircraft.

Aircraft A flies a distance of 962 miles in 2 hours.
Aircraft B flies a distance of 1644 miles in 3·5 hours.

Calculate the average speed of each aircraft, and say which one flew faster, on average.

E2 A freight train travels at a steady speed of 35 m.p.h.

(a) Calculate the time taken, in hours, to travel a distance of 168 miles. Give the answer in decimals.

(b) Change your answer to hours and minutes.

E3 It takes $1\frac{1}{4}$ hours to serve dinner on board a jet plane. The plane is travelling at 520 m.p.h. How far does it travel while dinner is being served?

E4 This diagram shows the timetable of a train from Edinburgh to King's Cross. The numbers in red are distances between stations, in miles.

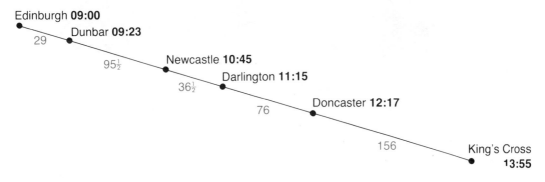

Edinburgh **09:00**
Dunbar **09:23**
29
$95\frac{1}{2}$
Newcastle **10:45**
Darlington **11:15**
$36\frac{1}{2}$
76
Doncaster **12:17**
156
King's Cross **13:55**

(a) How long does the train take to travel from Edinburgh to Dunbar? Give your answer in minutes.

(b) Change your answer to part (a) into a decimal of an hour.

(c) Calculate the average speed of the train between Edinburgh and Dunbar, to the nearest 1 m.p.h.

(d) Calculate the average speed of the train, to the nearest 1 m.p.h., between

(i) Dunbar and Newcastle   (ii) Newcastle and Darlington

(iii) Darlington and Doncaster   (iv) Doncaster and King's Cross

9

Money matters: income tax

The government spends a lot of money each year, on such things as education, health, defence, and so on. Much of this money comes from **income tax**. The amount which anyone has to pay depends on their income – the amount of money they have coming in.

People do not pay tax on the whole of their income. There is part of their income which they are allowed to keep without any tax being deducted from it. This part is called their **allowances**. The size of the allowances depends on a whole variety of things.

Your income
ALLOWANCES
taxable income
the Government
Your pocket

Find out

It is possible for someone to have an income and not pay any income tax.

Find out what is the most you can earn without having to pay tax.

The **rate** at which you pay tax depends on how much you earn.
Your taxable income (your income minus allowances) is 'sliced' into **tax bands**. Each band is taxed at a different rate.

10

This diagram shows the tax bands and tax rates in 1986–87.

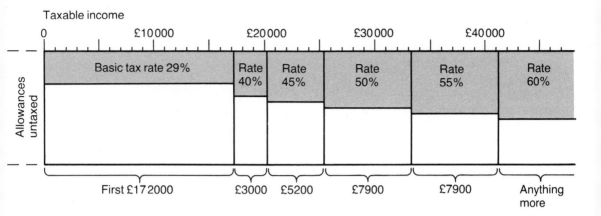

Find out

Find out what the tax bands are at the moment.

Work out how much tax is paid altogether by someone with a taxable income of £50000.

Tax facts

- The 'tax year' (the year for which your income is calculated for tax purposes) runs from 6th April in one year to 5th April in the next year.

  Before 1752, rents and taxes of all kinds were calculated up to the end of the first quarter of the year – 25th March, called 'Lady Day'.

  In 1752 an adjustment was made to the calendar, so that 2nd September was followed by 14th September. So from Lady Day 1752 to Lady Day 1753 there were only 354 days.
  The Treasury accounting system could not cope with that, so from 1753 taxes were collected 11 days later, on 5th April!

  When income tax was first introduced in 1799, 5th April was the date on which it was collected.

- For nearly 30 years in the 19th century there was no income tax. It started again in 1842. The rate was 3%!

- In 1875 the rate of income tax was down to 0·83%.

- The highest the (basic) rate has ever been was during the Second World War, when it was 50%.

- There are two small islands around the British Isles where no income tax is paid by the inhabitants – Lundy Island and Sark.

2 Value for money

A   Cost per kilogram, per litre, etc.

A shop sells apples in packs containing 3 kilograms.
The price of a pack is £1·59.

The cost of each kilogram of apples in the pack is

3 kg for
£1.59

$\dfrac{£1·59}{3} = £0·53$, or 53p.

The cost of 1 kg in the pack is called the **cost per kilogram**.
The cost per kilogram of this pack is **53p per kg**.

$$\text{Cost per kilogram} = \frac{\text{Price of pack}}{\text{Weight in kg}}$$

A1   Calculate the cost per kilogram, to the nearest penny, of each of these packs.

(a)   (b)   (c)

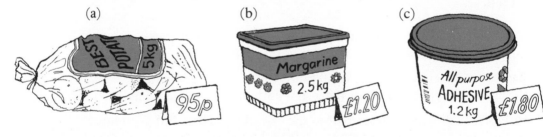

BEST POTATO 5kg   95p

Margarine 2.5 kg   £1.20

All purpose ADHESIVE 1.2 kg   £1.80

A2   Calculate the cost per litre, to the nearest penny, of each of these.

(a)   (b)   (c)

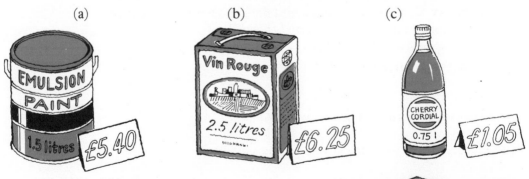

EMULSION PAINT 1.5 litres   £5.40

Vin Rouge 2.5 litres   £6.25

CHERRY CORDIAL 0.75 l   £1.05

A3   (a)   Calculate the area of this carpet.

       (b)   Calculate the cost per square metre
            of the carpet, to the nearest penny.

3·80 m   3·65 m

£99

Comparing prices (1)

A shop sells bars of chocolate in two sizes.
A 60 g bar costs 19p; a 100 g bar costs 29p.

60 g for 19p   100 g for 29p

Obviously the larger bar costs more, but is it better value for money?
One way to compare the prices is to calculate the cost of **1 gram** of
chocolate in each bar.

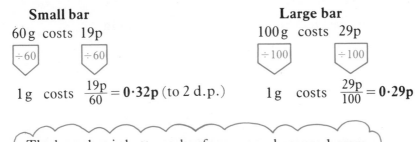

Small bar			**Large bar**	
60 g costs 19p			100 g costs 29p	
÷60	÷60		÷100	÷100
1 g costs $\frac{19p}{60} = \mathbf{0\cdot32p}$ (to 2 d.p.)			1 g costs $\frac{29p}{100} = \mathbf{0\cdot29p}$	

> The large bar is better value for money, because 1 gram
> of chocolate costs less in the large bar.

B1 One supermarket sells Class I new potatoes in 2 kg bags, costing
88p each. Another sells them in 3 kg bags, costing £1·28 each.

(a) Calculate the cost in pence of 1 kg of potatoes in the smaller bag.

(b) Calculate the cost of 1 kg in the larger bag.

(c) Which bag gives better value for money?

(d) Can you think of any reasons why people might buy the smaller
bag, even though it gives less 'value for money'?

B2 A 1·5 litre bottle of white wine costs £3·35 in one shop. Another
shop sells 2·5 litre bottles of the same wine for £5·75.

Calculate the cost of 1 litre in each of the two bottles.

B3 A timber yard sells lengths of wood for making shelves.
A 1·8 m length costs £2·55, and a 2·4 m length costs £3·25.

Calculate the cost per metre of each length.

Unit cost

The cost of 1 gram, 1 kilogram, 1 litre, etc., of something is called its **unit cost**. When things are sold in packs of different sizes, we can use unit costs to compare the prices.

Large packs do not always have smaller unit costs. Medium sized packs are often more popular with shoppers, so supermarkets can give greater discounts on them.

The smallest packs often have the highest unit cost, because the costs of packaging, handling and storing are high in relation to the cost of the contents.

B4 One item which shoppers buy in large containers is automatic washing machine powder.

Here are the prices in one supermarket for the different sized packs of two products.

Square Deal Surf		Bold	
870 g	75p	930 g	84p
3·41 kg	£2·17	3·1 kg	£2·59
6·2 kg	£3·94	4·65 kg	£2·99
		6·2 kg	£4·49

(a) Calculate the unit cost in **pence per kilogram** for each pack. Remember that 870 g is equal to 0·87 kg, and don't forget to change all the prices to pence.

(b) Which pack of Square Deal Surf has the lowest unit cost?

(c) Which pack of Bold has the lowest unit cost?

B5 Calculate the cost per square metre of each of these carpets, to the nearest penny, and find which carpet has the lowest cost per square metre.

(a)

(b)

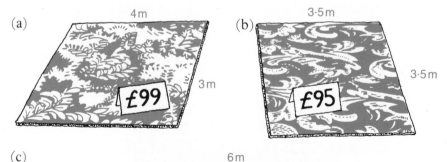

4 m
3 m
£99

3·5 m
3·5 m
£95

(c)

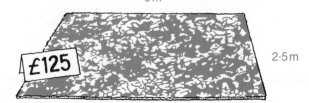

6 m
2·5 m
£125

c Comparing prices (2)

Here again are the two bars of chocolate shown on page 13.

We compared them by working out the **cost per gram** for each bar.
For the small bar it was **0·32p per gram**, and for the large bar **0·29p per gram**.

60 g for 19p   100 g for 29p

Another way to compare their prices is to work out how much chocolate
you get for 1p in each bar, like this:

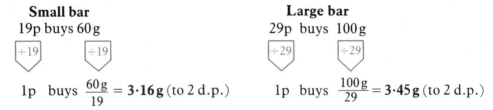

So the large bar gives you more chocolate for 1p than the small bar.

When we used the first method, on page 13, we were working out **the number
of pence you pay for 1 gram**.

When we use the method above, we are working out **the number of grams
you get for 1 penny**.

$$\text{Pence per gram} = \frac{\text{Price in pence}}{\text{Weight in grams}}$$ $$\text{Grams per penny} = \frac{\text{Weight in grams}}{\text{Price in pence}}$$

'Better value' means either **less pence per gram** or **more grams per penny**.

You can use either of the two methods to compare value, but you must be
clear which method you are using.

C1 Tins of rice pudding are sold in three sizes:

   213 g for 17p   439 g for 28p   624 g for 48p

  (a) Calculate the weight you get for 1p in each tin. Which tin
      gives the best 'value for money'?

  (b) Calculate the cost of 1 gram in each tin. Check that this method
      gives the same tin as 'best value'.

In questions C2 to C4, you can use either method of comparing prices.

Method 1   Calculate the unit cost (the cost of 1 kg, 1 litre, 1 gram, etc.).

Method 2   Calculate the amount you get for 1p or £1.

C2   Baked beans come in a variety of makes and sizes. Here are the prices charged in one supermarket.

Own brand (Co-op)   **Heinz**

220 g	12p	150 g	13p
439 g	15p	225 g	15p
539 g	25p	450 g	20p
		580 g	27p Family size
		840 g	38p Big family size
		2·62 kg	£1·35 Catering tin

(a) Using either method 1 or method 2, compare the prices of these tins.

(b) If you bought 6 of the 450 g tins, how much would it cost you?

(c) What would be the total weight of the 6 tins?

(d) Compare this with buying a single catering tin.

C3   A supermarket sells party cans of beer in two sizes. Their prices are as follows:

6·8 pints   £3·35
3·9 pints   £1·79

(a) Compare the 'value for money' of the two cans.

(b) Suppose you bought two of the smaller cans instead of one of the larger cans.

(i) How much extra beer would you get?

(ii) What would the extra cost be?

(iii) How much would you be paying per pint for the extra beer?

(c) Can you think of another reason (apart from 'value for money') for buying two smaller cans instead of the larger one?

C4   Coca-cola is sold in cans and bottles. Here are the prices in a shop.

Can	330 ml	17p	Bottle	1·5 litres	59p
Supercan	500 ml	26p	Bottle	2 litres	75p

(a) Compare the 'value for money' of these cans and bottles.

(b) Can you think of a reason why people might not prefer the 'best value' container?

Sometimes it may be more convenient to work out the **cost per 100 g** instead of the cost per gram.

C5 Here are the prices in a supermarket of various jars or tins of instant coffee.

50 g	64p	300 g	£3·25
100 g	£1·16	500 g	£5·99
200 g	£2·29		

The 50 g jar costs 64p. At this price, 100 g would cost **£1·28**.

(a) Calculate the **cost per 100 g** in the 200 g pack.

(b) Do the same for the 300 g pack.

(c) Do the same for the 500 g pack.

(d) Compare the 'value for money' of the five packs. Put them in order of value for money, best first.

(e) If you wanted to buy 1 kg of instant coffee for a big party, which of these would be cheapest?

Two 500 g tins	Three 300 g tins and one 100 g jar
Five 200 g jars	Ten 100 g jars

C6 These are the prices of various packs of crisps in a supermarket.

25 g	11p
75 g	26p
150 g	45p
250 g	65p
6 bags, each 25 g	57p
9 bags, each 25 g	79p

Every pack here is a multiple of 25 g. (In other words, every pack contains an exact number of 25 g 'units'.)

So we can compare the costs by working out how much we have to pay for 25 g in each pack.

For example, the 75 g pack contains 3 lots of 25 g and costs 26p.

So the cost of 25 g at this price is $\frac{26p}{3} = 8.67p$ (to 2 d.p.)

(a) How many lots of 25 g are there in 150 g?
What is the cost per 25 g in the 150 g pack?

(b) Work out the cost of 25 g in each of the other packs.

(c) What is the advantage of buying 6 bags, each 25 g, instead of a 150 g pack?

17

D Comparing prices in different shops

The table below shows the prices of various items in three different supermarkets.

(The information was collected in March 1984. It would be interesting to compare the prices then with what they are now.)

Item	Quantity	Price Supermarket A	Price Supermarket B	Price Supermarket C
Large white sliced loaf	1	34p	31p	32p
New Zealand butter*	250 g	52p	46p	50p
Margarine*	250 g	26p	24p	22p
Cheddar cheese	1 lb	£1·38	£1·22	£1·04
Eggs, size 3	6	44p	43p	50p
Milk	1 pint	21p	22p	21p
Streaky bacon	200 g	63p	63p	63p
Beef sausages	1 lb	63p	60p	59p
Lard	250 g	18p	15p	16p
Topside of beef	1 lb	£2·35	£2·08	£2·15
Neck of lamb	1 lb	68p	71p	66p
Belly pork	1 lb	88p	86p	87p
Chicken, frozen	1 lb	65p	62p	58p
Potatoes	1 lb	15p	18p	20p
Cabbage	1 lb	18p	24p	23p
Onions	1 lb	20p	21p	22p
Carrots	1 lb	18p	21p	25p
Tomatoes	1 lb	45p	48p	54p
Cooking apples	1 lb	28p	34p	27p
Eating apples (Gold. Del.)	1 lb	30p	29p	40p
Flour	1·5 kg	59p	34p	49p
Sugar	1 kg	45p	48p	51p
Instant coffee*	100 g	£1·35	£1·16	£1·19
Tea*	125 g	54p	44p	41p
Cornflakes*	250 g	48p	52p	47p
Jam*	1 lb	63p	55p	58p

A star against an item means that the price given is for the **same brand** in all three supermarkets.

You will notice that it is not always the same supermarket which is cheapest. For example, supermarket C is cheapest for margarine, but supermarket A is cheapest for potatoes.

One way to compare the supermarkets' prices is to make up a 'shopping basket' consisting of what a particular kind of person is likely to want. For example, a single person might want to buy these items in a typical week.

2 large white sliced loaves
250 g margarine
$1\frac{1}{2}$ lb Cheddar cheese
6 eggs
3 pints milk
1 lb beef sausages
2 lb potatoes
1 lb carrots
1 lb eating apples
125 g tea

D1 Work out the total cost of the 'shopping basket' above, in each of the three supermarkets.

Which supermarket is cheapest for this list of items?

D2 Work out the cost of each of these 'baskets' in each of the three supermarkets, and say which supermarket is cheapest.

(a) 5 large white sliced loaves
250 g butter
250 g margarine
3 lb Cheddar cheese
200 g streaky bacon
3 lb cooking apples
1 kg sugar

(b) 18 eggs
2 lb neck of lamb
250 g lard
3 lb potatoes
2 lb onions
1 lb tomatoes
1·5 kg flour

When people decide where to do their shopping, the prices are not the only thing they take into account.
For example, if the 'cheapest' shop is a long way away, the time and money spent in getting there and back may not be worth the savings made.

Project work

Make up a 'shopping basket' for either yourself or your family for a typical week.

Find out the price of each item in two different shops or supermarkets in your area.

Make a table showing the price of each item in the two shops.
Work out the total cost of the 'basket' in each of the two shops.

E Comparing prices over a period of time

The table below shows typical prices of various items in 1974 and in 1984.

Item	Quantity	1974 price	1984 price
Large white sliced loaf	1	14p	32p
Butter	250 g	12p	46p
Margarine	250 g	10p	22p
Cheddar cheese	1 lb	37p	£1·04
Eggs, size 3	6	15p	45p
Milk	1 pint	5p	21p
Streaky bacon	200 g	20p	63p
Beef sausages	1 lb	26p	59p
Lard	250 g	8p	17p
Topside of beef	1 lb	69p	£2·08
Neck of lamb	1 lb	39p	66p
Belly pork	1 lb	31p	87p
Chicken, frozen	1 lb	24p	58p
Potatoes	1 lb	3p	15p
Cabbage	1 lb	6p	18p
Onions	1 lb	8p	20p
Carrots	1 lb	7p	18p
Tomatoes	1 lb	14p	38p
Cooking apples	1 lb	10p	34p
Eating apples (Gold. Del.)	1 lb	16p	29p
Oranges	1 lb	12p	24p
Flour	1·5 kg	18p	40p
Sugar	1 kg	12p	46p
Instant coffee	100 g	39p	£1·16
Tea	125 g	11p	44p

Some price rises affect the cost of living more than others. A large increase in the price of something which people buy very little of may not have much effect.

For example, if smoked salmon or pheasant were to double in price, most people would not be affected. But if ordinary meat or vegetables go up in price, then this affects the cost of living much more.

We could compare the 1974 and 1984 prices item by item. But we get a much better idea of the overall increase in prices by using a 'shopping basket'. We put into the basket the items and quantities which a family buys in a typical week.

Here is a 'shopping basket' for a family of two adults and two children.

5 large white sliced loaves
250 g butter
$\frac{1}{2}$ lb cheese
12 eggs
250 g margarine
14 pints milk
200 g streaky bacon
1 lb topside of beef
1 lb neck of lamb
1 lb belly pork
$1\frac{1}{2}$ lb beef sausages
3 lb frozen chicken
16 lb potatoes
3 lb cabbage
2 lb onions
3 lb carrots
1 lb tomatoes
1 lb cooking apples
2 lb eating apples
$1\frac{1}{2}$ lb oranges
0·5 kg flour ($\frac{1}{3}$ of 1·5 kg bag)
250 g lard
1 kg sugar
25 g instant coffee ($\frac{1}{4}$ of 100 g jar)
125 g tea

E1 (a) Calculate the total cost of this shopping basket in 1974.

(b) Calculate the total cost in 1984.

E2 A prisoner is fed for a week on a 'punishment diet' of bread, margarine, cheese and milk. The amounts are:

5 loaves bread
250 g margarine
$\frac{1}{2}$ lb cheese
14 pints milk

(a) Calculate the total cost of feeding the prisoner in 1974.

(b) Calculate the total cost in 1984.

E3 Find out the present prices in a local shop of the items in the family basket above. Work out the cost of the basket at present prices.

3 Percentage

A Calculating a percentage of an amount

Each **percentage** has an equivalent **decimal**.

For example, 50% of something means the same as 0·5 of it.

The diagram on the right shows percentages from 0% to 100% with their decimal equivalents.

A1 Write down the decimal equivalent of each of these percentages.

(a) 35%   (b) 36%   (c) 59%   (d) 5%   (e) 8%

A2 Do not look at the scale! Write down the decimal equivalent of each of these percentages.

(a) 13%   (b) 3%   (c) 30%   (d) 72%   (e) 9%

Check your answers from the scale.

Worked example

Calculate 18% of £40.

To find 18% of something, we multiply it by the decimal equivalent of 18%, which is 0·18.

So 18% of £40 = 0·18 × £40 = **£7·20**.

A3 Calculate each of these.

(a) 65% of £90   (b) 32% of £70   (c) 14% of £60

(d) 7% of £80   (e) 3% of £250   (f) 60% of £98

Using your common sense

When you are calculating a percentage of something, it is useful to have a rough idea of what the answer should be.
It is useful to know that

50% of something is the same as 0·5 of it, or $\frac{1}{2}$ of it.

10% of something is the same as 0·1 of it, or $\frac{1}{10}$ of it.

So, for example, if you want 8% of £130, you know the answer will be a bit less than 10% of £130, which is £13.

Similarly, 63% of £130 will be a bit more than $\frac{1}{2}$ of £130.

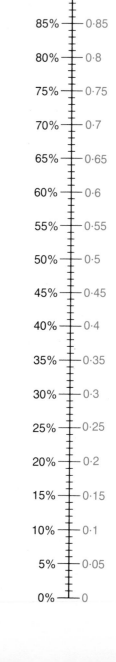

A4 Calculate each of these. Use your common sense to check that your answers are sensible ones.

(a) 45% of £66   (b) 11% of £850   (c) 9% of £140

(d) 32% of £550   (e) 7% of £240   (f) 73% of £660

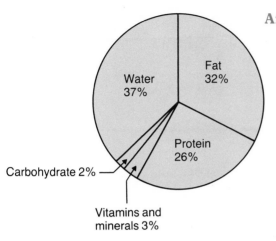

Water 37%

Fat 32%

Protein 26%

Carbohydrate 2%

Vitamins and minerals 3%

A5 This pie chart shows the composition of a particular kind of cheese.

Calculate the weight of each of these in 250 g of the cheese.

(a) Fat

(b) Protein

(c) Vitamins and minerals

(d) Carbohydrate

(e) Water

Check that the weights add up to 250 g.

B Percentage increases and decreases (1)

Increasing an amount by, say, 35% means adding on 35% of the amount.

Worked example

Increase £54 by 35%.

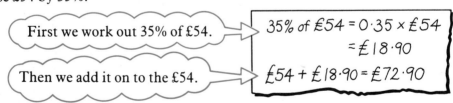

First we work out 35% of £54.

Then we add it on to the £54.

$35\% \text{ of } £54 = 0.35 \times £54$
$= £18.90$

$£54 + £18.90 = £72.90$

B1 A lorry driver gets paid £86 a week.
She asks for a wage rise of 12%. If she gets the rise, what will her new wage be?

B2 A trade union puts in a claim for a wage rise. They ask for an 8% rise for skilled workers and a 6% rise for unskilled workers.

The present wage rates are £8·50 per hour for skilled workers and £5·20 per hour for unskilled workers.

What would the new rates be (to the nearest penny) if both rises are granted?

B3 (a) Increase £64·60 by 30%.   (b) Increase £480 by 9%.
    (c) Increase £28·30 by 14%.   (d) Increase £62·65 by 8%.

23

Worked example

A shop has a sale in which prices are reduced by 15%.
What is the new price of an article whose original price was £48?

First we work out 15% of £48. → 15% of £48 = 0.15 × £48 = £7.20

Then we subtract this from the £48. → £48 − £7.20 = £40.80

B4 A company is doing very badly and may go out of business.
As a last desperate measure, it asks its workers to accept a
wage cut of 8%.

Calculate the wages which each of these workers would get if the
cut is agreed.

(a) A craftsman, at present paid £150 a week

(b) A technician, at present paid £120 a week

(c) An operator, at present paid £85 a week

(d) A part-time secretary, at present paid £42·50 a week

B5 (a) Reduce £90 by 20%. (b) Reduce £65·50 by 18%.

(c) Reduce £520 by 4%. (d) Reduce £6·90 by 45%.

B6 A company claims that its double-glazing and insulation will reduce
heating bills by 35%. A couple who at present pay £420 a year
for heating have their house double-glazed and insulated by the company.

(a) How much per year would they save if the company's claim is true?

(b) If the cost of the double-glazing and insulation is £2500, how
many years will it take them to save this much on heating bills?

C Expressing one amount as a percentage of another

Worked example

During a flu epidemic 136 children in a school of 318 were absent with flu.
What percentage of the children at the school were absent?

Write 136 out of 318 as a fraction.

Change the fraction to a decimal, by doing 136 ÷ 318.

Round off to 2 d.p.

Write it as a percentage.

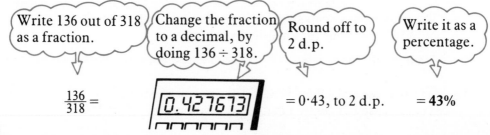

$\frac{136}{318} =$ 0.427673   = 0·43, to 2 d.p.   = 43%

C1 Express each of these as a percentage, to the nearest 1%.

(a) 47 out of 80   (b) 13 out of 35   (c) 26 out of 75   (d) 108 out of 780

C2 This is a map of a farm.
The areas of the fields are given in **hectares** (ha).
(1 hectare is equal to 10 000 square metres, about twice the area of a football pitch.)

Also shown on the map is
what each field is used for.

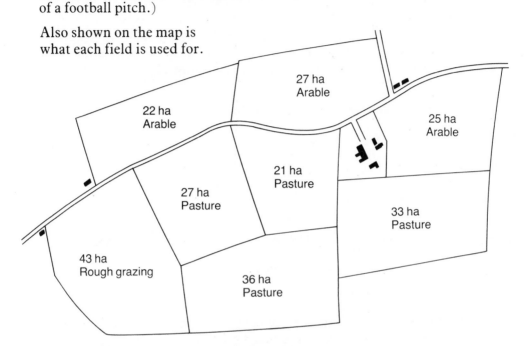

(a) Calculate the total area of all the fields.

(b) Calculate the area used for arable farming (growing crops).

(c) Calculate what percentage of the total area is used for arable farming.

(d) Calculate the percentage of the total which is used for rough grazing.

(e) Calculate the percentage which is used for pasture.

(f) Draw a pie chart to show how the farm is divided between
different uses.

C3 A survey of the ages of the people in a village produced these figures.

	Under 60	60 or over
Females	234	107
Males	268	73

(a) How many females are there in the village?

(b) What percentage of the females are aged 60 or over?

(c) What percentage of the males are aged 60 or over?

D Percentage increases and decreases (2)

Worked example

In April 1986, the population of a village was 245.
By the following April, it had gone down by 39.
What was the percentage decrease in the population?

A diagram helps to show what to do.

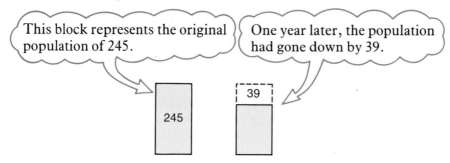

So the question is: what percentage of 245 is 39?

To get the answer, we do $\dfrac{39}{245} = 0\cdot159\,18\ldots = 0\cdot16$, to 2 d.p. = **16%**

So the population decreased by **16%** (to the nearest 1%).

(Check: 16% of 245 = $0\cdot16 \times 245 = 39\cdot2$.)

D1 A boutique had a sale. Before the sale, a dress cost £18.
In the sale, the price was reduced by £4.

What was the percentage reduction in the price, to the nearest 1%?

D2 The same boutique reduced the price of a pair of boots from
£45 to £37, a reduction of £8.

Calculate the percentage reduction in the price, to the nearest 1%.

D3 A camera shop reduced the price of a camera from £68 to £55.

(a) What was the actual reduction, in £?

(b) Calculate the percentage reduction, to the nearest 1%.

D4 Calculate the percentage reduction in each of these, to the
nearest 1%.

(a) From £31 to £25   (b) From £88 to £81

(c) From £420 to £375   (d) From £61·50 to £52·90

D5 Between 1986 and 1987, the membership of a club fell from
684 to 491. What was the percentage drop in membership?

Worked example

Jane's wages went up from £64 a week to £77 a week.
What was the percentage increase?

First of all we work out the actual increase.

Actual increase = £77 − £64 = £13

Once again, a diagram helps to show what to do.

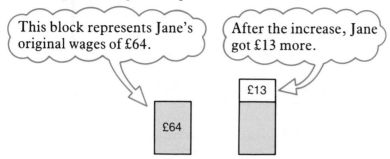

So the question is: what percentage of £64 is £13?

To get the answer, we do $\frac{13}{64} = 0\cdot2031 \ldots = 0\cdot20$, to 2 d.p. = **20%**.

So Jane's wages increased by **20%** (to the nearest 1%).

(Check: 20% of £64 = $0\cdot20 \times £64 = £12\cdot8$.)

D6   The price of a motorbike is increased from £760 to £810.
What percentage increase is that, to the nearest 1%?

D7   The population of a new town increased from 4300 to 4950.
What percentage increase was that, to the nearest 1%?

D8   Calculate the percentage increase in each of these, to the nearest 1%.

(a) From £40 to £53   (b) From £62 to £88

(c) From £95 to £99   (d) From £11·60 to £13·40

D9   Some of these are increases and some are decreases.
Calculate the percentage increase or decrease in each case,
and make it clear whether it is an increase or decrease.

(a) From £83 to £64   (b) From £26 to £33·50

(c) From £71·40 to £77·40   (d) From £38 to £33·40

D10 (a) The price of gas is increased from 32p to 36·5p per therm.
Calculate the percentage increase, to the nearest 1%.

(b) If electricity prices go up by the same percentage, what will
the new price be if the present price is 15·3p per unit?

E Mixed questions

E1 Calculate (a) 53% of £68 (b) 14% of £55

                       (c) 8% of £132 (d) 3% of £28

E2 (a) Increase £26 by 24%. (b) Reduce £340 by 18%.

     (c) Increase £65 by 7%. (d) Reduce £47 by 23%.

E3 Express each of these as a percentage, to the nearest 1%.

     (a) 37 out of 50 (b) 28 out of 36 (c) 19 out of 74

E4 Calculate the percentage increase when a price of £82 is increased to £98, to the nearest 1%.

E5 A shop reduces the price of a computer by 40%. Before the reduction the price was £185. What is the reduced price?

E6 A library contains 4260 books. At the end of the year it was found that 1554 books had not been taken out by anybody during the year. What percentage of the library's books had not been taken out?

E7 A disease reduced the population of a colony of animals from 234 to 188. Calculate the percentage decrease in the population.

E8 Last year a school fair raised £520 for charity. This year the fair raised £640. Calculate the percentage increase in the amount raised.

E9 A car manufacturer increases the price of all models by 12%. Calculate the new price of a car whose old price is £6794. Round off the price to the nearest £.

E10 Danny's pay was increased from £113 to £128 per week. Calculate the percentage increase in his pay.

E11 (a) Estimate what percentage of this strip is coloured. Write down your estimate.

     (b) (i) Measure the total length of the strip, in cm.
             (ii) Measure the length of the coloured part, in cm.
             (iii) Calculate what percentage of the strip is coloured. How close was your estimate?

4 Counting the cost

Sandra is 17, old enough to get a driving licence. She has saved up all the money from her weekend job, and wants to buy a car.

She sees an advert in a local paper for a car that she can afford.

> Austin 1100 L reg. Good cond.
> £150. Ring 431-0217 after 8pm.

She asks her mother what she thinks.

> **What do you think, Mum?**
> **Is it worth the price?**

> **I can't tell until I've seen the car.**
> **It could be a bargain, or it could be a load of old rubbish.**

> **Will you come and look it over for me?**

> **Hey, wait a minute! You can't even drive yet!**

> **I was hoping you could teach me.**

> **Well, perhaps I can. But what about the other costs? Can you afford them?**

> **What other costs? There's petrol, of course, but what else is there?**

> **Insurance, for a start. You're young and living in London, so that'll be about £200 a year.**

> **And there's your road fund tax. That's due to go up soon...**

> **... and it's an old car, so it'll almost certainly need some repairs doing...**

Working out the cost of something may involve more than you might think at first.

In the case of a car, there are **running costs** (road tax, insurance, petrol, oil, servicing, repairs, parking) as well as the cost of the car itself.

The next few pages contain examples of situations where it is a good idea to think carefully about the costs involved.

Buying your first camera

Most people who buy a camera do so to take holiday pictures, pictures of their family and friends, and so on. Some go on to become more interested in photography, and some may even make a living out of it.

Types of photograph

There are three types of picture you can take:

Colour prints   Colour slides   Black-and-white prints

Colour prints are the most popular. They are easy to carry around and show to people.

Colour slides generally give richer colours. But to see them you need either a hand-held viewer, or a projector and screen. With a projector you can get very large pictures.

Black-and-white prints are not so popular, now that colour prints are fairly cheap.

Films

Films are classified according to the type of picture they give. There are colour print films, colour slide films, and black-and-white print films.

All films, except those made for 'instant picture' cameras, have to be **processed** after they have been used in the camera.

When you buy a **colour slide** film, the cost of processing the film is usually included in the cost of the film. You are given an envelope to send the film away for processing. The slides come back to you through the post.

The processing of **colour print** and **black-and-white print** films has to be paid for separately. You have to send the film to a processing laboratory, or take it to a shop which sends films for processing. Different laboratories charge differently for processing, and quality varies. The cost will also depend on the size of the prints that you want. (Many keen photographers process their own films; to do this you need a darkroom and the necessary equipment.)

Processing of print films is done in two stages: **developing** and **printing**. The result of developing the film is a set of **negatives**. The pictures on the negatives are enlarged at the printing stage. Some processing firms charge for developing and printing separately.

Films are made with various different negative sizes, to fit different types of camera. Small negatives require more enlargement than large ones, so generally speaking you get sharper pictures from larger negatives.

Films are also made in different lengths, for example 12 exposures (pictures), 24 exposures, etc.

Types of camera

Cameras can be classified according to the size of film they take. There are five types which are suitable for beginners:

Disc   110   126   35 mm   Instant picture cameras

Disc cameras

These are small and flat and can fit into a handbag or pocket. The film which they use is mounted on a disc, which rotates inside the camera. Only colour print films are made for disc cameras.

110 size cameras

These are also small and take films in cassettes. The negative size is larger than that of a disc camera. Colour print and colour slide films are made in the 110 size.

126 size cameras

The negatives from this type of camera are square, and larger than the 110 size. Colour print and colour slide films are made in this size and, like the 110 films, are in easy-to-load cassettes.

Cameras of the three types above are easy to use and require no knowledge of photography.

35 mm cameras

There is an enormous range of makes and models of 35 mm camera, from very simple cameras which require no knowledge, to professional cameras. The negative size is a little larger than 126. Colour print, colour slide and black-and-white films are made in the 35 mm size.

35 mm cameras can be divided into two main types: **compact** and **single-lens-reflex** (SLR).

Compact cameras are small or fairly small, and most are easy for a beginner to use.

SLR cameras are generally more expensive than compacts, but many are just as easy to use. Their main advantage is that the lens can be taken off and replaced by others, such as 'wide-angle' lenses and 'telephoto' lenses. Wide-angle lenses allow the photographer to include more in the picture than the standard lens would include. Telephoto lenses allow less to be included, resulting in a 'close-up' effect.

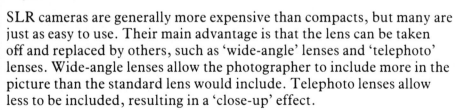

Standard lens   Wide-angle lens   Telephoto lens

Instant picture cameras

Instant picture cameras use a special kind of film which develops itself. After a picture has been taken, the print comes out of the camera.

Organising a disco

This is a checklist of what has to be done by the organiser of a disco.

1   You have to book a suitable hall (for example, a church hall).
    You need to have a date, and times for starting and finishing.
    Find out how much it will cost to hire the hall.

2   You need to book a mobile disco to provide the music and lightshow.
    Remember that the music must appeal to others, and not just to yourself!
    Find out how much it will cost for the mobile disco.

3   Design the tickets and posters and find out from printers how much
    they would charge for printing them.

4   Estimate the number of people who are likely to come to the disco.
    It is better to be pessimistic and under-estimate the numbers.
    Check the maximum number allowed in the hall by safety regulations.

5   Work out the total cost of the hall, the mobile disco, the tickets and posters.
    Add something for the cost of prizes. Then decide on the price of a ticket
    so that you break even, or make a profit if required.

6   Put the price on the ticket and poster design, and get these printed.

    Work out the amount of refreshments needed (for example, crisps and
    cola) based on the number of tickets for sale.

    Buy the refreshments. If you can, find a shop which will let you have
    them on 'sale or return'. This means that you can take unsold refreshments
    back to the shop and get a refund on them.

7   Distribute posters to people willing to display them (shops, etc.).
    Organise people to sell tickets.

8   Buy prizes for spot prizes and competitions.

9   Organise a committee of helpers to help on the day. They will need to

    (a) decorate the hall

    (b) collect tickets (and money?) at the door

    (c) serve refreshments (A 'float' is needed for change.)

    (d) act as 'bouncers'

    (e) clear up afterwards

    A rota for these jobs usually works well.

10 After the disco, you have to pay the bills and work out the profit (or loss).

Organising a camping trip

If you are organising a camping trip for about ten people, these are some of the costs you have to take into account.

Transport costs

You may decide to go to your holiday place by public transport, or you may decide to hire a minibus (if one of you is able to drive).

If you go by public transport, you can compare the costs of going by train or by coach.

While you are on holiday, you may want to travel around other than on foot. For example, there may be boat trips you can go on.

If you decide to hire a minibus, then you will need to know the cost of hiring it, and you will need to estimate the cost of petrol and oil.

The costs of hiring tents

If you need to hire tents, you need to know what size and how many you want, and find out the cost of hiring them.

Camp-site charges

You need to find out how much you will have to pay to use camp-sites.

The cost of food

You need to estimate what food you will need and how much it will cost. It may be cheaper to buy as much as possible before you go, but if you are going by coach for example, you may not be able to carry much food.

Food bought at camp-site shops or small local shops is sometimes more expensive than food bought in supermarkets.

Buying and running a motorbike

If you are thinking of buying a motorbike, these are some of the costs you have to take into account.

The cost of the bike itself depends on whether you buy new or secondhand.

The cost of insurance depends on the kind of insurance you have. (See page 59.)

The cost of clothing – helmet, gloves and suit.

The cost of extra equipment, for example a 'top box' or a waterproof cover.

The cost of learning to ride.

Running costs include road tax, the cost of petrol and the likely cost of repairs.

Buying and keeping a horse

These are the main costs involved in buying and keeping a horse.

The cost of the horse itself

The horse has to be of a suitable size for the person riding it.

The cost of paddock and stabling

During the summer, the horse can stay out in a field (provided there is some shelter). The owner of the field will charge for this.

During the winter, the horse is likely to need stabling, which has to be paid for.

The cost of food

During the summer, the horse will eat mainly grass, but can be fed oats and 'pony nuts'.

During the winter, the horse needs hay and bran with oats and/or pony nuts.

The cost of shoes

The frequency with which the horse's shoes are renewed depends on how much it is ridden. The horse's feet have to be 'dressed' (trimmed) every so often by a farrier, even if the shoes are not renewed.

The cost of tack

'Tack' includes the saddle, bridle, etc. needed for riding the horse.

The cost of grooming equipment

Brushes are needed for grooming the horse.

The cost of riding gear

To ride a horse you must have at least a hard hat.

The costs involved in entering for shows

If the horse is entered for a show, besides the entry fee there may also be the cost of hiring a horse box to take the horse to the show.

The cost of vetinerary treatment

If the horse should become unwell, it may need a vet, whose bills will need to be paid.

Keeping you

How much do **you** cost to keep?

The costs include the cost of housing, food, clothing, pocket money, presents, and many other things.

How much does it cost to keep you for a year?

Looking after a baby

What things does a very young baby need? How much do they cost (new or secondhand)?

How much money does a mother get in maternity benefit and child allowance?

Earning some extra money

Some young people who are still at school set up a small 'business' to earn extra money. The business may involve making and selling things, like children's toys or clothes, or it may involve doing services for people, like washing cars, digging gardens, decorating or perhaps typing.

Sometimes the hardest part of running a business like this is getting started: you have to provide something that people really want, not just something you think they want. And you have to find out how much they would be prepared to pay for it. You should aim to provide better quality or a cheaper service than they can get at present.

Some jobs may involve paying out money for equipment to start with. Remember that tools can often be hired quite cheaply by the day or by the week. (Even things like ladders and typewriters can be hired).

If you expect to use a lot of a certain item (for example, material for making soft toys) it is worth making sure that you are getting it from the cheapest supplier.

Once the business is going, there will be **income** (what you are paid) and **expenditure** (what you have to pay out).

After the business has been going for a while, you will have to compare your income with your expenditure. You will have to decide whether the amount of time you put into the business is worth the money and enjoyment you get out of it.

5 Maps and plans

A Plans

Portchester Castle lies on the north shore of Portsmouth Harbour, in
Hampshire. Parts of the castle were built by the Romans.

A plan of the castle is shown on the opposite page. The scale of the plan
is 1 cm to 20 metres.

A1   What are the buildings labelled A, B, C, D and E in the picture above?

A2   From which direction, roughly, was the picture taken?

A3   The picture was taken in winter.
Was it taken in the morning or the afternoon?

A4   The walls of the castle are roughly 9 m high.
Estimate the height of

(a) Land Gate   (b) the Keep

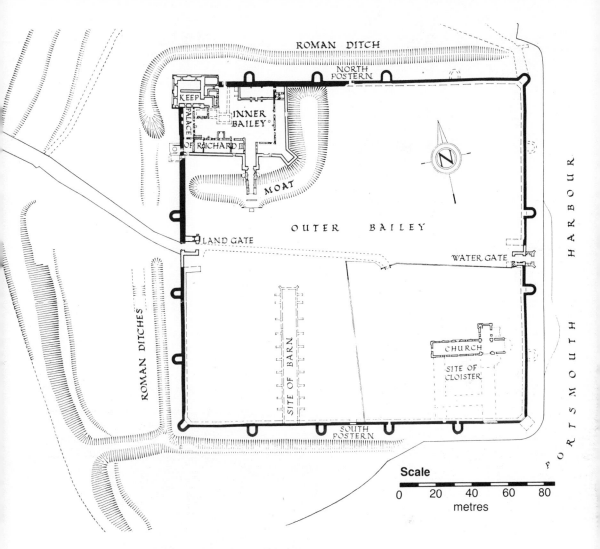

ROMAN DITCH

NORTH POSTERN

KEEP

PALACE OF RICHARD II

INNER BAILEY

MOAT

OUTER BAILEY

LAND GATE

WATER GATE

N

HARBOUR

ROMAN DITCHES

SITE OF BARN

CHURCH

SITE OF CLOISTER

SOUTH POSTERN

PORTSMOUTH

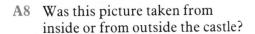

Scale

0   20   40   60   80

metres

A5 How long is the path between Land Gate and Water Gate?

A6 Estimate the total area inside the castle walls, in m².

A7 Estimate the area taken up by the church and its graveyard.

A8 Was this picture taken from inside or from outside the castle?

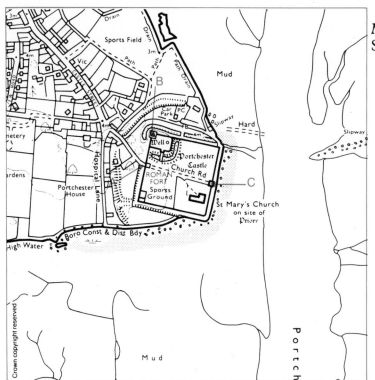

Map 1
Scale: 1 cm to 100 m

Map 2
Scale: 1 cm to 250 m

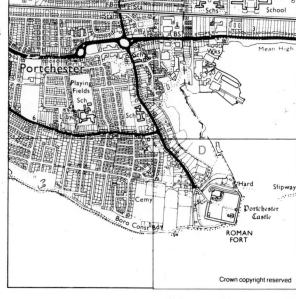

Map 3
Scale: 1 cm to ?

38

B Maps

Each of the maps on the opposite page shows Portchester Castle.
Notice that as the scale is reduced, less detail can be shown.

B1 (a) What are the features marked A, B and C on map 1?
   (b) How long is Hospital Lane?
   (c) Roughly how long would it take to walk the length of Hospital Lane?
   (d) There are two slipways marked on map 1. How far apart are they?

B2 (a) What is the place marked D in map 2?
   (b) What area, in km², does map 2 cover?

B3 (a) What is the feature marked E in map 3?
   (b) What is the scale of map 3?
   (c) Portchester station is marked —•— in map 3. How far is it on foot from the station to the castle?
   (d) Roughly how long would it take to walk this distance?
   (e) What area is covered by map 3?

On the right-hand edge of map 3 you can see part of a motorway junction.
An enlarged plan of the junction is shown below.

A car going from Southampton to Brighton passes the points F and H.

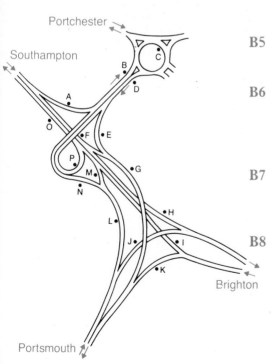

B4 A car is going from Portsmouth to Southampton. Write down the letters of the points it passes, in order.

B5 Where is a car going if it passes the point G?

B6 If you were travelling from Southampton and wanted to turn round and go back to Southampton, how could you do it? Which points would you pass, in order?

B7 How could you turn round if you were coming from Portsmouth and wanted to go back to Portsmouth?

B8 Which of these journeys **cannot** be done on this junction?

Portsmouth to Brighton
Brighton to Portsmouth
Southampton to Portchester
Brighton to Portchester

C Heights above sea-level

This picture shows an island.

All the points like A, B and C on the coast of the island are at **sea-level**.

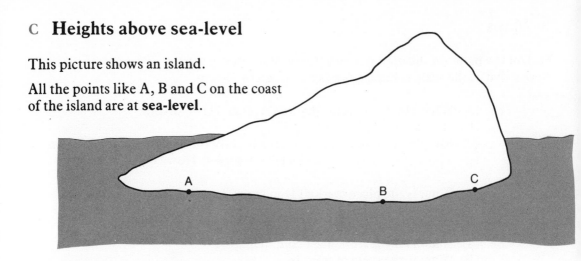

Imagine that the sea rises by 50 metres. The island will look like this.

All the points on the red line, like D, E and F, are 50 m above the original sea-level.

The red line is called the **50 m contour**. It goes right round the island.

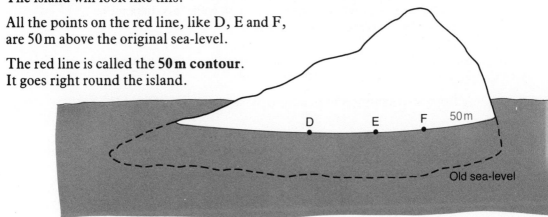

Imagine that the sea rises another 50 m. We get the **100 m contour**.

All the points on this contour are 100 m above the original sea-level.

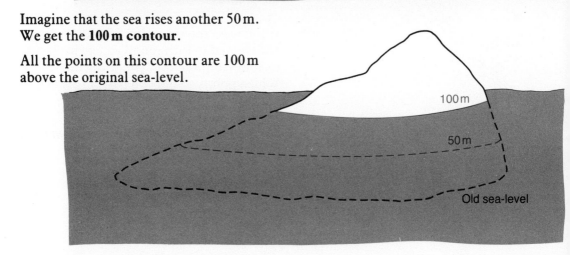

40

Imagine that the sea rises even further.
This picture shows the 150 m and 200 m contours.

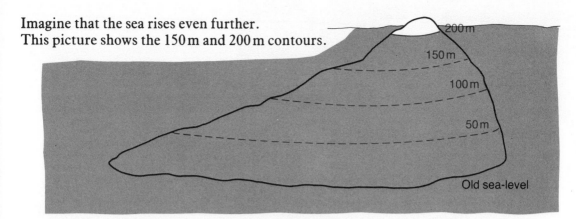

Here is a map of the island, with the sea back at its proper level.
The contours are shown on the map.

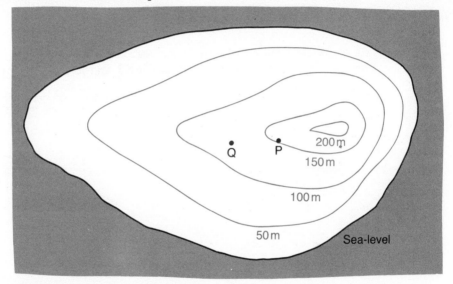

Contours are drawn on maps to show heights above sea-level.
For example, the point P on the map above is on the 150 m contour.
So P is 150 m above sea-level.

The point Q is between the 100 m contour and the 150 m contour.
So the height of Q above sea-level is probably between 100 m and 150 m.

People who use maps a lot can get a good idea of the shapes of hills
and valleys by just looking at contours.

> C1 How can you tell from the contours on the map that the
> left-hand part of the island is not so steep as the right-hand
> part?

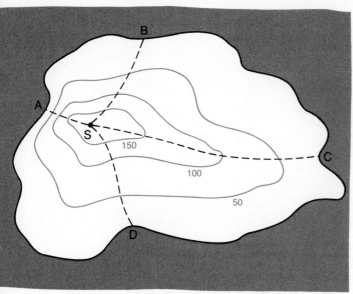

C2 This is a map of another island.

S is the highest point on the island.

There are four paths to S from points on the coast A, B, C and D.

(a) Which is the steepest path up to S?

(b) Which is the least steep of the four paths?

C3 The map below shows part of a country.
The contours show heights above sea-level, in metres.

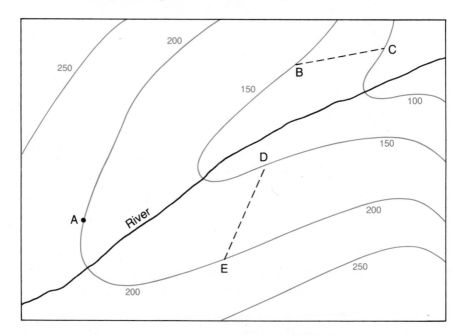

(a) How high above sea-level is the point marked A?

(b) Find B and C on the map. If you walk from B to C, will you be going **uphill** or **downhill**?

(c) Find D and E. If you go from D to E, will you be going uphill or downhill?

(d) Does the river marked on the map flow from left to right across the map, or from right to left?

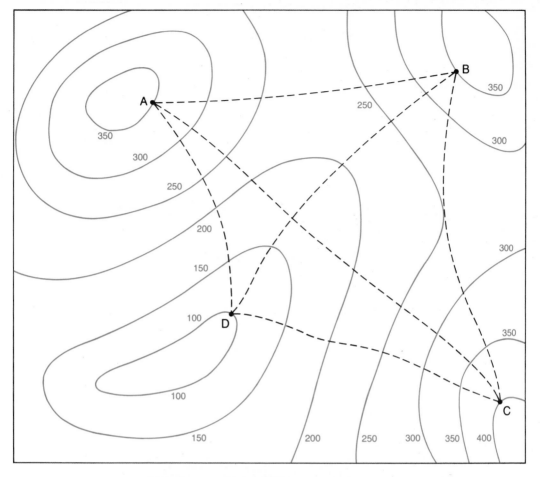

C4 The dotted lines on the map above are paths.

(a) Suppose you start at A and go along the path from A to B.
Your height at A is 350 m. Which contour lines do you
cross as you go from A to B? Write them down in the
order in which you cross them.

(b) Which of these four things do you do as you go from A
to B?

Go uphill all the way   Go downhill all the way
Go uphill first, then downhill   Go downhill first, then uphill

C5 Which of the four things listed in question C4 do you do
when you go from

(a) B to C   (b) B to D   (c) D to A   (d) C to A   (e) C to D

D Contours on OS maps

This is part of an Ordnance Survey map. The contours show heights in metres above sea-level.

Sometimes the height at a particular spot is marked. For example, in the square whose grid reference is 4843, a spot height of 119 metres is marked.

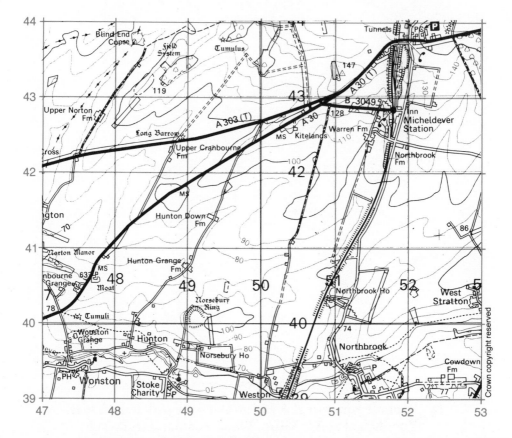

D1 Find Upper Cranbourne Farm on the map. Its grid reference is 488423. What is its height above sea-level?

D2 There is a long barrow near Upper Cranbourne Farm, and a track leads away from it in a north-easterly direction. Starting from the long barrow, does this track go **uphill** or **downhill**?

D3 Find the points whose grid references are 510430 and 475405. Imagine that you are driving along the main road between these two points. How does the road slope? (For example, is it downhill all the way?)

D4 Find Upper Norton Farm (reference 478427). Estimate its height above sea-level.

D5 Find Hunton Grange Farm. Give its grid reference and height.

1 Speed

1.1 A boat leaves Ambleside at 10:15 and arrives at Lakeside at 11:45.
The distance from Ambleside to Lakeside is 9 miles.
Calculate the average speed of the boat.

1.2 How long will it take to travel 135 miles at a speed of 54 m.p.h.?

1.3 A plane travels at 116 m.p.h. for $1\frac{3}{4}$ hours. How far does it travel
during that time?

1.4 A company plans to run a hydrofoil service from Weymouth to
Guernsey, a distance of 84 miles. The hydrofoil travels at
a speed of 32 m.p.h. Calculate the journey time in hours and
minutes, to the nearest 10 minutes.

1.5 This diagram shows the route and timetable of a coach service.

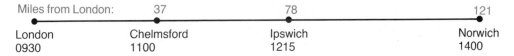

Miles from London:	37	78	121
London 0930	Chelmsford 1100	Ipswich 1215	Norwich 1400

(a) Calculate the average of speed of the coach between London and
Chelmsford.

(b) (i) How far is it from Chelmsford to Ipswich.

    (ii) How long does the coach take to get from Chelmsford to Ipswich?
Give the time in **hours**, not hours and minutes.

    (iii) Calculate the average speed of the coach between Chelmsford and
Ipswich?

(c) Calculate the average speed of the coach between Ipswich and Norwich.

2 Value for money

2.1 A shop sells lager in two kinds of pack:

    4 bottles, each 275 ml, cost 85p   4 cans, each 440 ml, cost £1·25

(a) Find the total quantity of lager in the 4 bottles. Write the
quantity in **litres**.

(b) Calculate the cost per litre of the lager in the 4-bottle pack.

(c) Calculate the cost per litre of the lager in the 4-can pack.

(d) Which pack offers better value for money?

3 Percentage

3.1 Calculate   (a) 30% of £250   (b) 40% of £170

(c) 18% of £160   (d) 9% of £130

3.2 Car prices go up by 14%. Calculate the new price of a car which cost £5064 before the increase.

3.3 Express each of these as a percentage, to the nearest 1%.

(a) 43 out of 60   (b) 38 out of 90   (c) 173 out of 410

3.4 Janice started a 'Keep Fit' club at her school. To start with there were 34 members. After a year the membership had increased to 47. Calculate the percentage increase in the membership.

3.5 88 people go on a package holiday. 23 of them are dissatisfied with the hotel. What percentage of the people are dissatisfied?

3.6 The price of a 100 g jar of coffee goes up from £1·20 to £1·35. Calculate the percentage increase in the price, to the nearest 1%.

5 Maps and plans

5.1 This map shows a motorway junction.

(a) Which lettered points do you pass if you are travelling

(i) from Dartford to Reigate

(ii) from Reigate to Tonbridge

(iii) from Reigate to Maidstone

(b) Which of these journeys **cannot** be done on this map?

Dartford to Tonbridge
Dartford to Maidstone
Maidstone to Tonbridge
Tonbridge to Maidstone

5.2 Which is the steepest side of this island, the north, south, east or west side?

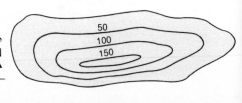

6 Rates

A Rates

The pump on a modern fire engine can deliver about 4500 litres of water in 1 minute.

We say the **rate** at which the water comes out is **4500 litres per minute**, and we write it 4500 litre/min.

Rates are always measured in 'somethings per something'.
Here are some other examples of rates:

(1) The rate of working of a newspaper printing machine is about **45 000 copies per hour**.

(2) An experienced typist can type at a rate of about **60 words per minute**.

(3) When you go up a mountain, the temperature falls at a rate of about **0·6 °C per 100 metres**.

(4) A medium-sized car on a long journey uses up petrol at a rate of about **9 litres per 100 km**.

A1 A central heating boiler burns gas at the rate of 750 cubic feet per hour. If it is left burning for 24 hours, how many cubic feet of gas will it use up?

A2 In good driving conditions on a motorway, Petra's car will do 45 miles per gallon of petrol. The petrol tank has 7 gallons in it. How far will Petra be able to go before she runs out of petrol?

A3 A garage charges for labour at a rate of £14·50 per hour. What is the total labour charge for a repair which took $6\frac{1}{2}$ hours to do?

A4 Patrick is paid at a rate of £4·40 per hour during normal working hours and at a rate of £6·40 per hour for overtime.
   (a) How much is he paid for 42 hours of normal working and $3\frac{1}{2}$ hours of overtime?
   (b) One week Patrick earned £236. He worked 42 hours at the normal rate. How much overtime did he do?

Calculating rates

Worked example

Maureen took $8\frac{1}{2}$ minutes to take down 550 words in shorthand.
What is her rate in words per minute?

> Think of how you calculate a speed in **miles per hour**: you divide the number of **miles** by the number of **hours**.
> So to calculate a rate in **words per minute**, you divide the number of **words** by the number of **minutes**.
>
> Maureen's rate $= \frac{550}{8 \cdot 5} = \textbf{65 words per minute}$ (to the nearest whole number)

Most of the rates we calculate are **average** rates. In the worked example above, Maureen's average rate is 65 words per minute. We do not expect her to write exactly 65 words in each 1 minute.

A5 Keith typed 360 words in 8 minutes.
Calculate his rate in words per minute.

A6 Sadia drove 126 miles on $3\frac{1}{2}$ gallons of petrol. Calculate the average number of miles per gallon.

A7 Calculate the rate of flow in litres per minute for each of these taps. Give each answer to the nearest litre per minute.

(a) A tap which fills a 600-litre tank in 9 minutes

(b) A tap which takes 17 minutes to fill a 200-litre tank

A8 A freshwater spring takes 5 minutes to fill a 2-litre bottle.
Calculate the rate of flow of the spring, in litres per minute.

A9 A typist is paid £99 for 36 hours' work. What is his rate of pay per hour?

A10 The rate at which a person's heart is beating can be found by taking their pulse.

A nurse took a patient's pulse. She counted the number of beats during a period of 15 seconds. She counted 19 beats.

Calculate the patient's pulse rate in beats per minute.

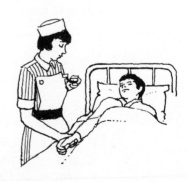

A11 Calculate the pulse rate of a person whose heart beat 28 times in 20 seconds. Give the rate in beats per minute.

B Calculations involving rates

Worked example

An aircraft is using up fuel at the rate of 45 litres per minute.
There are 7500 litres of fuel in the aircraft's tank.
For how much longer will the aircraft be able to fly?

> In 1 minute the aircraft uses 45 litres.
> We have to find how many times 45 litres goes into 7500 litres,
> and that will tell us how many minutes the aircraft will fly.
>
> So we divide 7500 by 45. $\quad \dfrac{7500}{45} = 166 \cdot 66 \ldots$ minutes
>
> $\qquad\qquad\qquad\qquad\qquad = 167$ minutes, to the nearest minute
>
> $\qquad\qquad\qquad\qquad\qquad = \textbf{2 hours 47 minutes}$

B1 It says on the label of a tin of paint that 1 litre will cover about 15 m^2. How many litres will be needed to cover the walls of a room if their total area is 120 m^2?

B2 A printer wants to print 10 000 copies of a leaflet.
She starts the printing machine. After 5 minutes it has printed 700 copies.
  (a) Calculate the rate of printing, in copies per minute.
  (b) How long will it take altogether to print 10 000 copies?

B3 The turntable of a record player is supposed to rotate at a rate of $33\frac{1}{3}$ revolutions per minute.

Debbie counted 158 revolutions in 5 minutes. Is the turntable running at the correct speed, or too slow, or too fast?

B4 Paul is painting a fence, which is 40 metres long. After working for $1\frac{1}{2}$ hours, he has painted 12 metres. How much longer will it take him to paint the rest, if he works at the same rate?

B5 Pat is crossing the desert in a truck. She starts with a full fuel tank holding 140 litres of fuel. After travelling 80 miles, she has used up 25 litres.

She still has 390 miles to go. Will she make it? Explain how you got your answer.

B6 A company operates a ferry service between England and the continent. At present they use ships which have a speed of 18 m.p.h., and the journey takes $3\frac{1}{2}$ hours.

They plan to replace the ships by hydrofoils which have a speed of 30 m.p.h. How long will the journey take?

Money matters: VAT

The things which people spend their money on can be divided up into **goods** and **services**.

'Goods' are the things you buy from shops or mail order firms, such as food, clothes, records, computers, and so on.	'Services' are things that other people do for you, such as repair your bike or TV set.

VAT is a tax which is charged on most goods and services.
The tax goes to the government to help pay the cost of running the country.

For some goods you do not have to pay VAT. Examples are books and take away cold foods.

DUMPLINGS PRICE LIST		
	Eat here	Take out
Plain · · · · · · 80p		70p
Beef · · · · £1·03		90p
Apple · · · · ·86p		75p
Banana · · · 92p		80p

The rate of VAT is fixed by the government. The rate may be changed from time to time. If there is a change, it is usually announced in an annual Budget in March.

Suppose the rate of VAT is 15%. You want to buy a bike whose price excluding VAT is £80.
If you buy the bike you will be charged £80 + 15% of £80 = £80 + £12 = **£92**.

1 Find out the present rate of VAT. Work out the cost, including VAT, of an item whose price excluding VAT is

(a) £10 (b) £20 (c) £50 (d) £55 (e) £58·50

Suppose you are in business. You buy materials, from which you make things to sell to other people.

You pay VAT when you buy the materials, but **you get this back from the taxman**.

What happens is illustrated in this story.

The story: Alan sells Brenda the wood to make a dog kennel.
Brenda makes the kennel, and sells it to Colin, who paints it.
Diana buys the kennel from Colin.

The rate of VAT at the time is 10%.

Brenda buys the wood from Alan.
Alan charges £20 + VAT = **£22**.

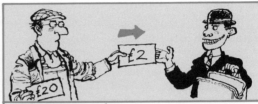

Alan keeps £20.
He pays £2 VAT to the taxman.

Colin buys the kennel from Brenda.
Brenda charges £60 + VAT = **£66**.

Brenda keeps £60.
She pays the £6 VAT to the taxman.
She gets back the £2 VAT she paid on the wood.

Diana buys the kennel from Colin.
Colin charges £100 + VAT = **£110**

Colin keeps £100.
He pays the £10 VAT to the taxman.
He gets back the £6 VAT he paid on the kennel.

At each stage the taxman collects 10% of the **value added** to the kennel.
For example, Colin buys it for £60 and sells it for £100.
The value added is £40, so the taxman gets £4 from Colin. (Colin gives him £10 but gets £6 back.)

At the end of the story, the taxman has made a gain of £10, which is 10% of the final selling price of the kennel.

7 Mixing and sharing

A Mixing in a given ratio

Sadia and Tina open a shop called 'The Pink Pyjama Shop'.

They decide to paint the inside of the shop in various shades of pink.
They have been given tins of red paint and tins of white paint, so they decide to mix red and white together to get pink.

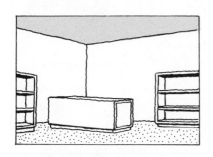

They want to paint the ceiling a very light shade of pink. They decide to mix red and white paint in **the ratio 1 to 3**. This means that for every 1 litre of red paint they use 3 litres of white.

A1 How much white paint would they mix with

(a) 2 litres of red   (b) 5 litres of red   (c) 3·5 litres of red

A2 How much **red** paint would they mix with

(a) 12 litres of white   (b) 18 litres of white   (c) 1·5 litres of white

Sadia wants the walls to be painted in a deeper shade of pink than the ceiling. Tina suggests mixing red and white in the ratio 2 to 3, and this is what they decide to do.

For every 2 litres of red they use 3 litres of white.

A3 For the walls, how much white paint would they mix with

(a) 4 litres of red   (b) 8 litres of red   (c) 10 litres of red

The basic 'recipe' for the colour of the walls is **2 litres red to 3 litres white**.

Sadia works out other combinations which give the same colour. She does it by multiplying or dividing the basic recipe.

For example, doubling the basic recipe gives **4 litres red to 6 litres white**.
Halving the basic recipe gives **1 litre red to 1·5 litres white**, and so on.

Worked example

If the ratio of red to white is 2 to 3, how much red should be mixed with 12 litres of white?

The basic recipe is: 2 litres red to 3 litres white
If we want to use 12 litres of white, we have to multiply the basic recipe by 4, because 3 litres × **4** = 12 litres.

Basic recipe: 2 litres red to 3 litres white

$\times 4 \downarrow \qquad \times 4 \downarrow$

8 litres red to 12 litres white

So we have to mix **8 litres of red** with 12 litres of white.

> **A4** The ratio of red to white is 2 to 3.
> (a) How much white should be mixed with 6 litres of red?
> (b) How much red should be mixed with 24 litres of white?
>
> **A5** (a) How much white should be mixed with 5 litres of red?
> (b) How much red should be mixed with 4·5 litres of white?

Tina and Sadia want the furniture to be a very deep pink.

They mix red and white in the ratio **4 to 3**.

> **A6** For the furniture, how much white paint would they mix with
>
> (a) 8 litres of red
>
> (b) 20 litres of red
>
> **A7** The ratio of red to white is 4 to 3.
>
> (a) How much white should be mixed with 12 litres of red?
>
> (b) How much red should be mixed with 12 litres of white?
>
> **A8** Tina wants to paint the doors a deeper shade of pink than the furniture.
> Suggest a ratio of red to white which she could use.

53

Suppose Sadia and Tina are making their very light pink colour.
The recipe for it is 1 litre of red to 3 litres of white.

The recipe will make **4 litres** of pink paint altogether.

1 litre red and 3 litres white → 4 litres pink

Suppose they need 20 litres of pink paint.
They will have to use **5 times** the basic recipe, that is
5 litres of red and 15 litres of white.

A9   Tina mixes red and white in the ratio 1 to 3.
She wants to make 12 litres of pink paint.
How much red and how much white will she need?

A10   Sadia is mixing paint for the walls. She mixes red and
white in the ratio **2 to 3**.
How much red and how much white will she need to make

(a) 10 litres of pink   (b) 25 litres of pink   (c) 2·5 litres of pink

(d) 20 litres of pink   (e) 30 litres of pink   (e) 1 litre of pink

A11   For the furniture, the ratio of red to white is **4 to 3**.
How much red and how much white will be needed to make

(a) 21 litres of pink   (b) 3·5 litres of pink   (c) 35 litres of pink

B   Sharing in a given ratio

Sadia and Tina open their shop. It is open for 5 days a week.
Sadia works in the shop 2 days a week and Tina 3 days a week.

They decide to share the profits of the shop in the ratio 2 to 3.

We want our shares to be in the ratio 2 to 3. How do we work them out?

Let's split the profits into 5 equal parts.

Why 5 equal parts?

PROFITS

Sadia   Tina

Because then you can have 2 parts and I'll have 3 parts. So our shares will be in the ratio 2 to 3.

In the first week after opening, the profits are £120.
Sadia and Tina share the profits in the ratio 2 to 3.

They split the £120 into 5 equal parts: $\frac{£120}{5}$ = £24.

Sadia gets 2 parts, which is $2 \times £24 = £48$.
Tina gets 3 parts, which is $3 \times £24 = £72$.

They check that their shares add up to £120:   £48 + £72 = £120.

B1   In the second week, the profits are £300. Sadia and Tina share
     them in the ratio 2 to 3. Work out their shares.

B2   In the third week, the profits are £420. Share them between
     Sadia and Tina in the ratio 2 to 3.

After a while they decide to open the shop 6 days a week.
Sadia still works 2 days a week, but Tina now works 4 days a week.

They decide to share the profits in the ratio 2 to 4.

(Tina's share will be twice Sadia's share, so the ratio can also be
written as '1 to 2'.)

B3   Sadia and Tina share a profit of £480 in the ratio 2 to 4 (or 1 to 2).
     Calculate their shares.

B4   Share each of these amounts between Sadia and Tina in the
     ratio 2 to 4 (or 1 to 2). Give the shares to the nearest penny.

     (a) £183   (b) £517   (c) £209   (d) £272·50

B5   The rent of the shop goes up. To help pay it, the two girls decide
     to open 7 days a week. Sadia works 3 days a week and Tina
     works 4 days a week. They share the profits in the ratio 3 to 4.

     Calculate their shares to the nearest penny when the profits are

     (a) £252   (b) £146   (c) £316·25   (d) £173·38   (e) £216·09

B6   Pink pyjamas suddenly become fashionable. Sadia and Tina
     make a timetable for working in the shop. Sometimes both of
     them are working together.

	Mon	Tues	Wed	Thurs	Fri	Sat	Sun
Sadia	✓				✓	✓	✓
Tina		✓	✓	✓		✓	✓

(a) How would you suggest they should share the profits?

(b) Calculate their shares when the profits are £351·40.

C Sharing between three

Ken, Colin and Diane earned £540 between them by decorating a flat.
Ken worked for 2 days, Colin for 3 days and Diane for 4 days.
They decide to share the £540 between them in the ratio **2 to 3 to 4**.

$2 + 3 + 4$ is equal to 9. So they first split the £540 into **9 equal parts**.

Each part is $\frac{£540}{9} = £60$.

Ken gets 2 parts, which is $2 \times £60 = £120$.
Colin gets 3 parts, which is $3 \times £60 = £180$.
Diane gets 4 parts which is $4 \times £60 = £240$.

$$\underline{£540}$$

Check: all three shares add up to £540.

C1 Kate, Cheryl and Pauline cleared a garden of rubbish, weeded it and dug it over. Here is a record of who worked when.

	Mon	Tues	Wed	Thurs	Fri
Kate	✓	✓		✓	
Cheryl	✓		✓	✓	✓
Pauline		✓	✓		✓

Altogether they earned £450. Suggest how they should share it out, and work out their shares.

C2 Manoj, David and Ronnie re-wired a house and agreed to share the amount they earned in the ratio 3 to 4 to 5.
They earned £300 altogether. Calculate their shares.

C3 A light green paint can be made by mixing blue, yellow and white paint in the ratio 3 blue to 4 yellow to 1 white.

How much of each of the three colours is needed to make 20 litres of light green paint?

Concrete

Concrete is made from cement powder, sand and gravel.
The cement, sand and gravel are mixed with water, but the water dries out later as the concrete 'sets'.

Each type of concrete can be described by giving the ratios, or **proportions**, of cement, sand and gravel.
One commonly used concrete is called '1 to 3 to 6' concrete.
The proportions here are by **volume**: 1 bucketful of cement is mixed with 3 bucketfuls of sand and 6 bucketfuls of gravel.

When the concrete is mixed, the total volume decreases by about one-third.

D Miscellaneous problems on mixing and sharing

D1 PVA glue is very popular for gluing wood and other materials. It can also be mixed with water for other purposes. The information below comes from the label of a tin of PVA glue.

Purpose	PVA	Water
Sealing dusty ceilings and floors	1	5
Priming gloss paint before wallpapering	1	1
Sealing end-grain wood	5	1
Stiffening fabrics	1	19

(a) How much water should be mixed with 250 ml of PVA when stiffening fabric?

(b) A floor needs 30 litres of mixture to seal it. How much PVA and how much water are needed?

(c) 15 litres of mixture are needed to prime some gloss paint before wallpapering. How much PVA and how much water should be used?

(d) A carpenter decides to make up 3 litres of mixture for sealing end-grain wood. How much PVA and water are required?

D2 Here is an extract from Grandma's will.

> I leave £600 to my grandchildren Ruth and David, to be divided between them in the ratio of their ages when I die.

(a) Now Ruth is 3 years old and David is 2 years old. What will they each get if Grandma dies now?

(b) In one year from now, Ruth will be 4 and David 3. What will they each get if Grandma dies one year from now? Give the amounts to the nearest penny.

(c) Suppose Grandma dies five years from now, when Ruth is 8 and David is 7. How much will each child get?

(d) Suppose Grandma dies when Ruth is 13 and David 12. Work out the amounts each child will get.

D3 Karen and Judith set up a health food shop. Karen puts £2000 into the business and Judith £2500. They agree to share the profits in the ratio of the amounts they put in.

The shop makes a profit of £180 in the first month. How much will each person get?

Money matters: Insurance

Holiday medical insurance

If you go abroad for a holiday, you may fall ill or have an accident, and need medical treatment.

Medical treatment is often expensive abroad.

So it is a good idea to **insure** yourself against medical expenses.

To do this, you pay a fairly small amount of money, called a **premium**, to an insurance company. The company then agrees to pay any medical expenses which may arise on your holiday, up to a certain amount.

Here for example are the premiums charged by the 'Globule Insurance Co.' for different lengths of holiday.

Globule Insurance	10 days	20 days	30 days
Medical £1000	£1·50	£2·75	£4·00
expenses £5000	£5·00	£8·50	£11·50
up to £10000	£8·00	£14·50	£19·50

Why is the insurance company willing to do this? They know, from past experience, that most holidaymakers do not fall ill or have accidents on holiday. So most of the people who pay their premiums will not need to have medical expenses paid for them.

The company tries to fix the premiums so that it can pay the expenses of the few people who do need treatment out of the total of all the premiums paid in. It also makes sure that there is enough left over to pay the costs of running the business, and make a profit.

Insurance companies know from experience that in some parts of the world a holidaymaker is more likely to need medical treatment than in others. So the premiums for these places are higher.

   1   Insurance companies generally have higher premiums for winter sports holidays than for summer holidays. Why is this?

Car and motorcycle insurance

Motorcyclists and car drivers are required by law to be insured.
There are three main types of insurance they can have.

(1) **Third party.** If the driver (or rider) is involved in an accident in which another person is injured or killed or another vehicle damaged, the insurance company pays any compensation, and the cost of any repairs to the other vehicle.

(2) **Third party, fire and theft.** The insurance company also pays if the driver's own vehicle is damaged by fire or stolen.

(3) **Comprehensive.** The company also pays for the repairs to the driver's own vehicle if it is damaged in an accident.

The premium which the driver pays depends on a number of things:
the type of insurance; the driver's age and occupation; where the driver lives; the make, model and age of the car or motorbike.

Different companies have different premiums, so it is a good idea to shop around to get the best deal.

The premium covers one year's insurance. If the insurance company does not have to pay out anything during that year, then it usually gives the driver a **no claims discount** on his or her next year's premium.
Here is an example of the 'no claims discounts' offered by one company.

1 year's claim-free insurance	25% discount
2 years' claim-free insurance	40% discount
3 years' claim-free insurance	50% discount
4 or more years' claim-free insurance	60% discount

This means the driver pays 25% less than the normal premium.

If the company has to pay out during a year's insurance, the driver loses two years' discount. (So 60% discount becomes 40%, 50% becomes 25%.)

2   Janice is 22 years old, lives in Birmingham and drives an 8 year old Ford Escort 1300.

In her first year of driving she was comprehensively insured and paid the normal premium of £180.

She is a very careful driver, and she made no claim during that year (so the insurance company did not have to pay out anything). So she was allowed a 25% no claims discount on her premium for the second year.

(a) If the normal premium was still £180, what did Janice have to pay in her second year?

(b) Janice made no claim during her second year and she is now going to insure for her third year. The insurance company allows her a 40% no claims discount. The company has increased all its premiums, so the normal premium is now £210. What will Janice have to pay?

8 Graphs and charts

A Bar charts

Tuberculosis is a very serious disease, usually affecting the lungs. It is much less common now than it was in the past, thanks largely to vaccination.

This table shows the number of cases of tuberculosis in Britain in various years.

Year	1921	1931	1941	1951	1961	1971
Number of cases	85 000	83 000	70 000	60 000	26 000	13 000

Most people find it easier to 'take in' information like this if it is presented in the form of a picture.

Here is a **bar chart** which shows the information.

You can see very clearly the huge drop in the number of cases between 1951 and 1961. (The BCG vaccination was introduced in 1954.)

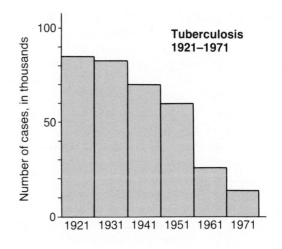

A line graph can also be used to show the same information.

The dotted lines on this graph are there just to help the eye. You cannot use this graph to find the number of cases between the years given.

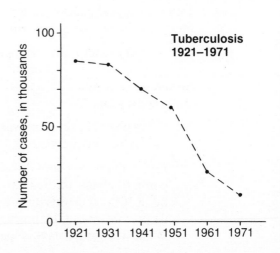

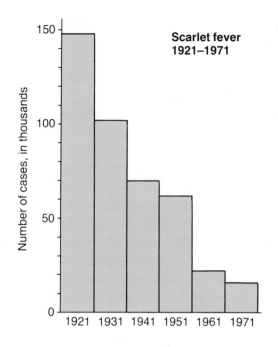

Scarlet fever 1921–1971

Number of cases, in thousands

A1 This bar chart shows how the number of cases of scarlet fever dropped between 1921 and 1971.

(a) Estimate from the chart the number of cases in 1921.

(b) Estimate the number of cases in 1931.

(c) Estimate the number of cases in 1971.

We can estimate percentage decreases (and increases) from a bar chart.

Here for example are the bars for 1931 and 1941 from the chart above.

We imagine the 1931 bar split into 10 equal parts. Each part is 10% of the 1931 bar.

We can see that the 1941 bar is about 70% of the 1931 bar.
So there was a **30% decrease** in scarlet fever cases between 1931 and 1941.

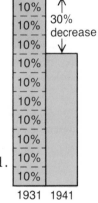

A2 Estimate from the chart above the percentage decrease in scarlet fever cases between 1921 and 1931. (Estimate to the nearest 10%.)

A3 Estimate to the nearest 10% the percentage decrease in scarlet fever cases between

(a) 1941 and 1951   (b) 1951 and 1961

A4 Use the chart on the opposite page to estimate the percentage drop in the number of cases of tuberculosis between 1951 and 1961.

A5 Use the figures in the table on the opposite page to calculate the percentage drop in tuberculosis cases between 1951 and 1961, to the nearest 10%.

The diagram below consists of two bar charts put together.
One bar chart shows the populations of the major urban regions of England.
The other shows their areas.

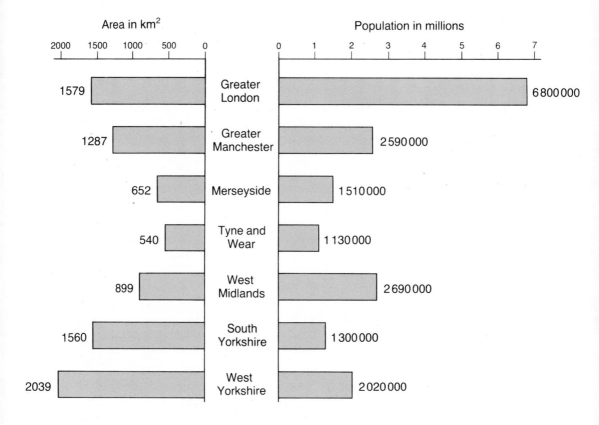

Major urban regions of England

A6 (a) Which of the regions in the chart has the largest population?

(b) Which has the smallest area?

From the chart you will see that Greater Manchester and the West Midlands have roughly the same population, but the area of the West Midlands is quite a bit smaller.

We can compare these two regions by calculating their **population densities**, which are measured in **people per square kilometre**.
To do this, we divide a region's population by its area.

The population density of Greater Manchester is $\frac{2\,590\,000}{1287} = 2012$ people per km^2
(to the nearest whole number).

So, in Greater Manchester, there are 2012 people for each square kilometre of space.

62

A7 Calculate the population density of the West Midlands, and compare it with that for Greater Manchester.

A8 (a) Calculate the population densities of the other regions in the chart. Make a table of population densities, showing the seven regions in order of population density, highest first.

(b) Draw a bar chart to show this information.

A9 This chart gives information about eight English counties.

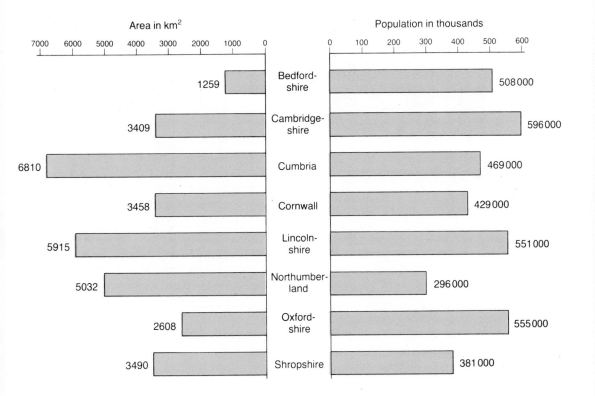

(a) Without doing any calculations, can you pick out the county which is most densely populated? It is the one whose population is the largest **in relation to its area**.

(b) Can you pick out the county which is least densely populated?

(c) Calculate the population density of each of the eight counties, and arrange the counties in order with the most densely populated first.

B Misleading charts

Sometimes people use charts to mislead others.

When you look quickly at this chart, it looks as if this month's sales are about double last month's.

When you look at the scale at the side of the chart, you can see that it does not start at 0.

If the whole chart is drawn, it looks like this. Sales have increased, but **not** doubled.

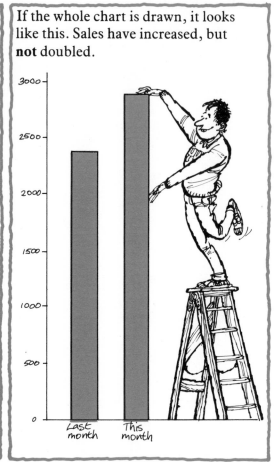

If you draw a bar chart whose scale does not start at 0, it is better to draw broken bars, like this. (Unless, of course, you want to mislead!)

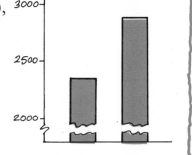

B1 This chart shows a firm's profits in 1986 and 1987.

Why is the chart misleading?

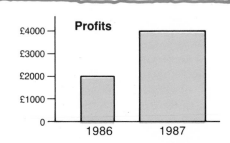

Charts are often made to look more like pictures.
Sometimes the pictures can be misleading.

B2 A bakery increased its sales of loaves from 300 000 in November to 900 000 in December. So the December sales were 3 times the November sales.

Which of these two charts gives a fairer picture of the increase, and why?

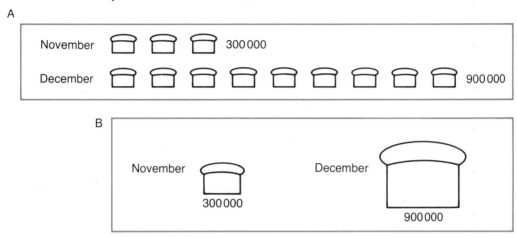

A

| November | 300 000 |
| December | 900 000 |

B

November 300 000

December 900 000

B3

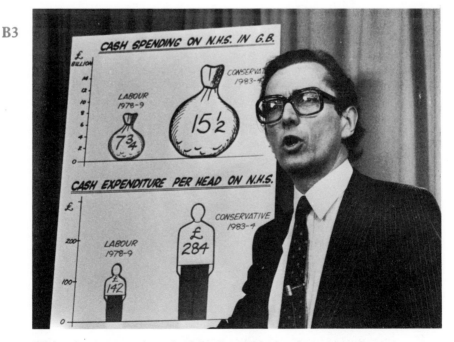

This photo was taken during the 1983 election campaign.
It shows the Minister of Health and Social Security with charts showing increases in spending on the National Health Service.
Do the charts give a fair picture of the figures?

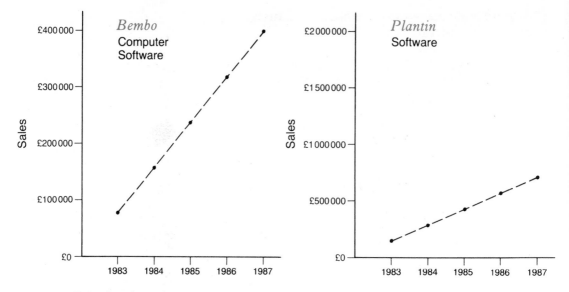

B4 Look at the two graphs above.
Which of the two businesses is growing faster?

B5 Why is the graph below misleading?

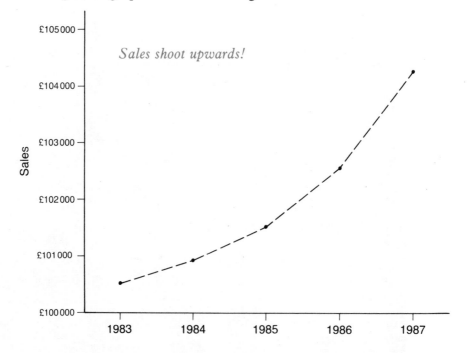

Sales shoot upwards!

B6 Imagine that you own a business. Your sales figures for the past five years have been £20 000, £25 000, £28 000, £27 000, £27 500.

Draw a chart which shows how well you have done. You don't have to use all the figures.

Money matters: Foreign exchange

When you travel abroad, you need to have foreign currency.

In France, you need French **francs**, in Italy you need **lire**, in Spain **pesetas**, etc.

You can 'buy' foreign currency from a bank or 'bureau de change'. The amount you get for every pound is called the exchange rate.

Exchange rates vary from day to day. Over long periods they may change quite considerably.

BUREAU DE CHANGE	
FRANCE	11·86
ITALY	2350
SPAIN	225
GREECE	151
GERMANY	3·89
HOLLAND	4·36
AUSTRIA	27·25
USA	1·45
CANADA	1·80

1   If the exchange rates are as shown in the picture above, how many French francs would you get for   (a) £50   (b) £80

2   How much would you have to pay (in £) for 500 francs?

3   In France, a restaurant advertises three set menus, costing 35F, 54F and 72F. Calculate the cost of each of these in pounds and pence.

Travellers' cheques are a good way to take money abroad. You can change them for money when you get there. Each cheque is for your own personal use only, and if you lose one you do not lose any money, provided you report the loss quickly.

Travellers' cheques can be issued in £ sterling, US dollars, French francs, etc.

When you change money, the bank or bureau de change charges you a small amount (called 'commission') for the transaction.

When you leave the foreign country, or when you get home, you may have some foreign money left. If you go to change it back into Sterling, you will find that the exchange rates for changing foreign money into Sterling are slightly different from the rates for changing Sterling into foreign money. From your point of view the rates are slightly worse: you don't get back quite as much as you would expect.

6 Rates

6.1 The volume of water in a reservoir fell from 17 400 litres to 12 600 litres during a period of 5 days.

(a) Calculate the rate of emptying, in litres per day.

(b) After how many more days will the reservoir be completely empty, if the water continues to flow out at the same rate?

6.2 A car's engine does 32 miles per gallon of petrol.

(a) How far will the car travel on $8\frac{1}{2}$ gallons of petrol?

(b) How many gallons would be used up travelling 200 miles?

6.3 A 60-watt light bulb uses up electricity at the rate of 0·06 units per hour. The bulb is left on over a weekend, from 6 p.m. on Friday evening until 9 a.m. on Monday morning.

(a) For how many hours was the light bulb left on?

(b) How many units of electricity did it use up?

(c) How much did the electricity cost, if 1 unit costs 5p?

7 Mixing and sharing

7.1 Rosie and Chris have a shop. Rosie works 3 days a week and Chris 2 days, so they agree to share the profits in the ratio 3 to 2.

(a) How much does each of them get when the profits are £160?

(b) One week, Chris's share of the profits came to £34. What was Rosie's share?

(c) Another week, Rosie's share was £84. What was Chris's share?

7.2 There are two schools in a small town. One has 250 children and the other 150 children.
A local businessman dies and leaves £6000 to be spent on equipment for the two schools. The schools agree to divide the money between them in the ratio of the numbers of children in the schools.

(a) Express the ratio 250 to 150 in its simplest form.

(b) Divide the £6000 between the schools in this ratio. Write down the amount each school will get.

8 Graphs and charts

8.1 This graph shows how much protein is eaten per day, on average, in three different parts of the world.

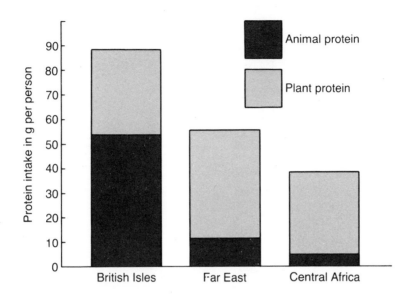

Estimate the percentage of animal protein in the daily protein intake in each of the three parts of the world.

8.2 Criticise the poster shown on the left.

8.3 Criticise the chart shown below.

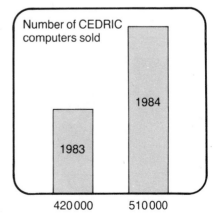

9 Squares and square roots

A Square roots

The **square** of a number is that number multiplied by itself.
The square of 3 is 3×3 (written 3^2), which is 9.

It is called the **square** of 3 because a square
with sides 3 units long has an area of 3×3
or 9 square units.

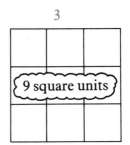

3

3 | 9 square units

A1   What is the square of   (a) 6   (b) 7   (c) 8   (d) 9   (e) 10

A2   Use a calculator to find the square of
(a) 23   (b) 57   (c) 405   (d) 836

A3   Use a calculator to work out   (a) 47^2 (b) 325^2 (c) 500^2

9 is the square of 3. We say 3 is the **square root** of 9.

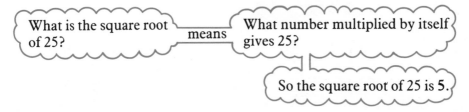

What is the square root of 25?   means   What number multiplied by itself gives 25?

So the square root of 25 is 5.

A4   Write down the square root of   (a) 36   (b) 4   (c) 81

A5   Copy these sentences. Fill in the missing numbers.

(a) 8×8 is . . ., so 8 is the square root of . . .

(b) The square of 10 is . . ., so 10 is the square root
of . . .

(c) 7×7 is . . ., so . . . is the square of . . ., and
. . . is the square root of . . .

B The squares graph

Here is a table of numbers from 0 up to 8, with their squares.

Number	0	1	2	3	4	5	6	7	8
Square of number	0	1	4	9	16	25	36	49	64

If these values are plotted on a graph, we find that the points all lie on a smooth curve.

The graph can be used to find **squares** and **square roots**, as shown.

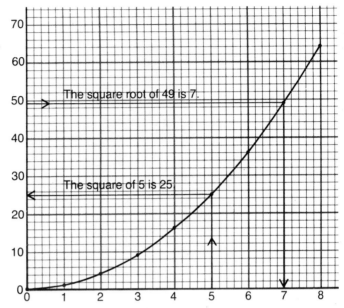

The square root of 49 is 7.

The square of 5 is 25.

B1 (a) What does one small square **across** stand for?

(b) What does one small square **up** stand for?

B2 (a) You can find a rough value for the square root of 40 from the graph, like this.
Find 40 on the up axis. Go across from there until you get to the curve, then go down to the across axis. Read off the number there. Write down the result.

(b) Use a calculator to multiply your number by itself. See if the answer is close to 40.

B3 Use the graph to find a rough value for the square root of 30. Multiply the number by itself. See if the answer is close to 30.

B4 (a) Extend the table at the top of this page to include the squares of 9 and 10.
Draw the graph yourself, with numbers across from 0 to 10.

(b) Use your graph to find a rough value for the square root of 75.

(c) Use a calculator to multiply your rough value by itself. The answer should be close to 75.

Money matters: Saving

Most people save up for their holidays or Christmas, or for something special.
But where do they keep their savings? Under the mattress, in tins, etc.

Money left around the house is not very safe.
And as prices rise, the money will buy less and less.

The money could be put into a bank deposit account, or a Post Office Savings account, or a building society account, etc.

When you save money in this way, the bank or building society etc. pays you for leaving your money with them. The amount they pay you is called **interest**.

Why is the bank willing to do this? The reason is that the bank lends the money to other people, who pay the bank even more interest than the bank pays you. In that way the bank covers its costs and makes a profit.

Banks and building societies have various savings schemes, each with its **annual interest rate**, given as a percentage.

Suppose the interest rate is 10% per annum. 'Per annum' means 'per year', so your savings would grow by 10% each year.

	£
1st June 1987	80·00
Interest 87–88	+ 8·00
1st June 1988	88·00

For example, suppose you put in £80 on 1st June 1987.

You leave the money in for 1 year. It earns interest which is 10% of £80, or £8.

On 1st June 1988, your savings have grown to £88.

10% of £80

If you leave the £88 in for another year, the interest you will get for that year is **10% of £88**, or £8·80.

This is what the savings account looks like if the money is left in and none is taken out.

	£	
1st June 87	80·00	
Interest 87–88	+ 8·00	
1st June 88	88·00	
Interest 88–89	+ 8·80	10% of £88·00
1st June 89	96·80	
Interest 89–90	9·68	10% of £96·80
1st June 90	106·48	

1 Rajesh puts £500 into a savings account on 1st June 1987.
The interest rate is 8% p.a. (p.a. stands for per annum).

The statement, or record, of his account starts like this.

	£
1st June 87	500·00
Interest 87–88	+ 40·00
1st June 88	540·00

The first year's interest is 8% of £500. To work out 8% of something, you divide by 100 (to get 1%) and multiply by 8.

Or you can just multiply by **0·08**.

Continue the statement until 1st June 1991.

2 Pauline puts £200 into a savings account on 1st September 1987.
The interest rate is 12% p.a.

Write out a statement of Pauline's account up to 1st September 1990.

3 Stan was given £500 when his uncle died.
He wanted to buy a motorbike, which cost £750.

He worked out that if he put his money into a savings scheme, after five years he would have £750, and be able to afford the bike.

Why is he likely to be disappointed?

73

Suppose £500 is deposited (paid) in a savings account, and the interest rate is 10% p.a.

Each year the amount grows by 10%. This diagram shows how the amount grows.
(The amounts are rounded off to the nearest £.)

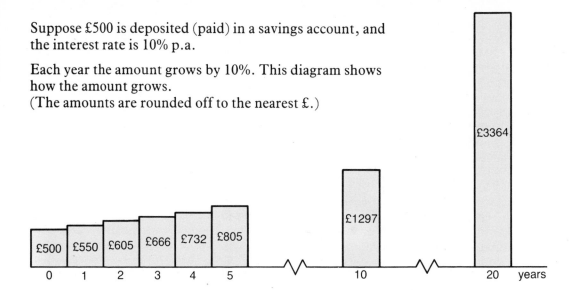

If prices are also rising at the same rate, 10% per year, then although the amount in the savings account grows, it will not be worth any more than it was to start with.

In practice, interest is often calculated monthly, and added on monthly. But if you want to compare two savings schemes and how well they pay, the **annual percentage rate** of interest is what you have to look at.

All savings schemes are required by law to state their annual percentage rate (or APR, for short).

Regular savings

Some savings schemes offer a higher APR if you agree to pay in a certain amount regularly, for example every month.

Premium bonds

Premium bonds do not pay any interest. Instead of interest you get what is in effect a raffle ticket, which may win a prize. You have in effect paid for the raffle ticket with the interest which you would have got if you had put the money into a savings scheme.

You can 'cash in' premium bonds, and get back the same amount as you paid for them. But in the meantime prices may have gone up. In that case the same amount of money would be worth less than when you first bought the bonds.

10 Arranging and selecting

A Timetables

Young people come to an adventure holiday centre for five days.
The warden divides them into three groups, A, B and C.
There are five activities, and each group does a different one each day.

Water safety

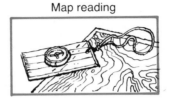

Map reading

Hill walking

Canoeing

Athletics

The warden makes a chart like this. He has filled in the week's activities
for one of the groups.

	Monday	Tuesday	Wednesday	Thursday	Friday
Group A	Map reading	Water safety	Canoeing	Hill walking	Athletics
Group B					
Group C					

There are three rules for planning the activities:

- Every group must do water safety before it does canoeing.
- Every group must do map reading before it does hill walking.
- Two or more groups cannot be doing the same activity on the same day.

> A1 Copy the warden's chart. Put in the activities he has planned
> for group A. Check that they obey the first two rules.
>
> Now complete the chart for the other groups, making sure that
> you obey all three rules.
> You may have to try different arrangements before you find one
> that obeys all the rules. So work in pencil, or cut out pieces of
> paper with the activities written on them and move them around
> on your chart until you have a plan that works.

A2 Five students, Rachel, Sadia, Kevin, Martin and Peter, go on a five-day craft course. Each student has to spend three of the days in the pottery. There is room in the pottery for only three students at a time.

Copy this chart. Rachel's days in the pottery are already filled in.

Complete the chart.

	Day 1	2	3	4	5
Rachel	✓	✓			✓
Sadia					
Kevin					
Martin					
Peter					

A3 Four people work in an office. Each one gets 3 weeks' holiday, but not more than 2 weeks can be taken in any one stretch.

They all have to take their holidays within a period of 6 weeks, but not more than two of them are allowed to be away at the same time.

(a) Two people, Janet and Rajesh, have already fixed up their holidays, as in this chart.

	Week 1	Week 2	Week 3	Week 4	Week 5	Week 6
Janet	✓	✓		✓		
Rajesh	✓	✓				✓
Patrick						
Gillian						

Can the other two people arrange their holidays without breaking the rules? If so, show how it can be done.

(b) If Rajesh moves his one week from week 6 to week 5, can Patrick and Gillian arrange their holidays without breaking the rules? If so, show how it can be done.

A4 Five basketball teams, A, B, C, D and E, decide to have a tournament.
Each team has to play every other team once.
Each team has to have at least one game's rest between playing.

For example, they might start like this:

1st game	2nd game	3rd game
A plays B. C, D and E rest.	C plays D. A, B and E rest.	. . . . . .

Make a chart like this and use it to plan the tournament. (You do not have to start with teams playing as shown here.)

When you think you have finished, check that each team has played every other team.

76

B Choosing pairs

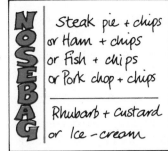

Karl decides to go to the Nosebag café every day for lunch. The menu is always the same. There is a choice of four main courses and a choice of two puddings.

Karl wants to see how many days he can go to the café without ever having **exactly** the same meal twice.

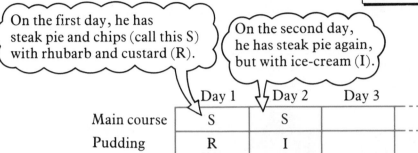

On the first day, he has steak pie and chips (call this S) with rhubarb and custard (R).

On the second day, he has steak pie again, but with ice-cream (I).

	Day 1	Day 2	Day 3
Main course	S	S	
Pudding	R	I	

B1 Copy the table and continue it.
How many days can Karl go to the café without ever having exactly the same meal twice?

B2 Helen goes to Stavros's restaurant every day for lunch. The menu is shown on the left.

Helen is more fussy than Karl. She never has the same main course two days running, and she never has the same pudding two days running.

For example, if she has fish and chips with trifle on one day, she will not have either of them the next day.

(a) Make a plan showing what meals Helen could have for seven days, if she never has exactly the same meal twice.

(b) Could Helen eat at the restaurant for more than seven days without having two identical meals? What is the longest she could do this?

B3 Hema has four jumpers, one red (R), one blue (B), one green (G) and one yellow (Y).
She has three skirts, orange (O), cream (C) and lavender (L).

(a) Hema never wears the same jumper two days running or the same skirt two days running. Show how she could go for ten days without wearing exactly the same outfit twice.

(b) If she does this for ten days, has she used all the different possible outfits? How many outfits are there altogether?

c Picture cards

The four cards on the opposite page come from a set of 24 cards.
They were made in Germany about a hundred years ago.

(The cards here have been lettered to make it easy to refer to them.)

The cards are designed so that any two of them placed side by side
will 'join up' to make a single picture.
This means that you can make many different pictures by rearranging
the cards.

For example, here are two of the different pictures you can make
starting with the lighthouse (card P) on the left.

PQRS

PQSR

C1   What other pictures could you make with the four cards starting
with card P on the left? Write them out using the letters.

C2   See how many pictures you can make starting with the rock (Q)
on the left.

C3   (a)   How many different pictures can you make with the tree (R)
on the left?
     (b)   How many different pictures could be made altogether with
the four cards?

There are 24 cards in the full set. The number of different pictures you
could make using all 24 cards is over 620 000 000 000 000 000 000 000.

P

L. 12 L.

Q

K. 1 A.

R

L. 2 B.

S

K. 18 R.

79

The cards on the opposite page come from another set made about 150 years ago.

They can be arranged in various ways to make different 'characters'.

C4 Here are 24 different characters which can be made from the cards on the opposite page. But there are three more possible characters that are not shown here.
See if you can work out which ones are missing.

A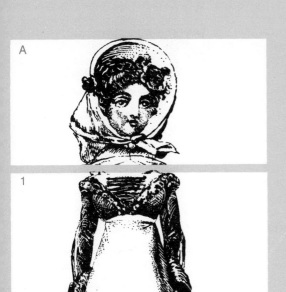

B

1

2

X

Y

C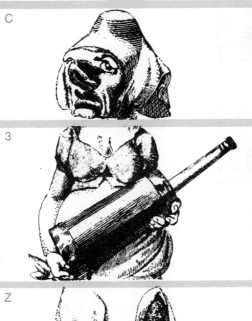

3

Z

D Listing possibilities

Here is another lunch menu.

Suppose we want to make a list of all the different meals it is possible to have.

We could try just writing them down in any old order, until we couldn't think of any more.
But it is better to have a **method** for making a list, so that we can be **sure** that none have been left out.

One good method is to use a **branching diagram** (also called a **tree diagram**).

This is how it works.

The Gravy boat

Lamb chop & 2 veg.
or Shepherd's pie & 2veg.
or Hamburgers & 2 veg.
_____
Apricot pie & custard
or Jelly & cream
or Banana Split

---

1 We show the three choices of main course like this.
(L stands for 'lamb chop', etc.)

L

S

H

2 L (lamb) can be followed by A (apricot), J (jelly) or B (banana). We show them like this.

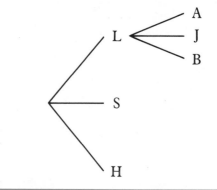

---

3 S can be followed by A, J or B.
H can be followed by A, J or B.
We show them like this.

4 Now we can list all the possible meals by following the lines across the diagram.

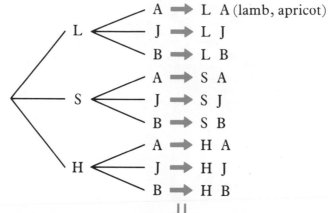

L ⟨ A → L A (lamb, apricot)
    J → L J
    B → L B

S ⟨ A → S A
    J → S J
    B → S B

H ⟨ A → H A
    J → H J
    B → H B

9 possible meals altogether

D1 (a) Make a branching diagram to show all the possible meals which can be chosen from this menu.

Start like this:

Fish and chips
or Sausage and chips
or Cheese salad
or Ham salad
_____
Treacle pudding
or Apple pie

(b) Use your diagram to make a list of all the different possible meals. The list begins   F T   F A   . . .

KB90

available in R ed
Y ellow
G reen
B lue

MODELS AVAILABLE :

S aloon

H atchback

E state

D2 People who want to buy the new KB90 car have a choice of four colours: red, yellow, green or blue.

They also have a choice of three models: saloon, hatchback or estate.

(a) Copy and complete this branching diagram, to show all the possible combinations of colour and model.

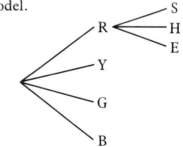

(b) Make a list of all the possible combinations. How many are there?

D3 The new RX75 car comes in a choice of three colours: W (white), B (blue), O (orange).

There is a choice of two models: S (saloon), H (hatchback).

There is a choice of two engines: 1·3 litre, 1·6 litre

(a) Copy and complete the branching diagram.

(b) How many different possible combinations are there?

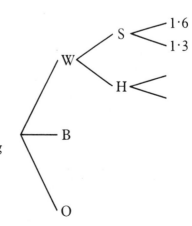

11 Fractions

A Halves, quarters, eighths, ...

Some British firms still use inches for measuring lengths.

This line is 1 inch long: |——————|

The symbol for inches is ". So 3" means 3 inches.

To measure lengths which are shorter than 1", an inch can be divided in half, then in half again, and again, and so on.

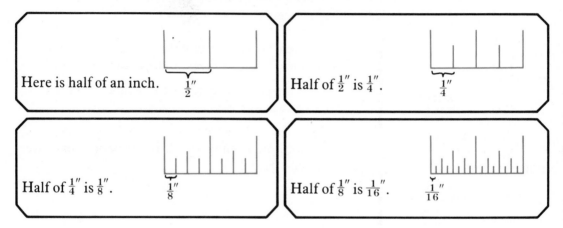

Here is half of an inch. $\frac{1}{2}''$

Half of $\frac{1}{2}''$ is $\frac{1}{4}''$. $\frac{1}{4}''$

Half of $\frac{1}{4}''$ is $\frac{1}{8}''$. $\frac{1}{8}''$

Half of $\frac{1}{8}''$ is $\frac{1}{16}''$. $\frac{1}{16}''$

This enlarged diagram of an inch shows all the halves, quarters, and so on.

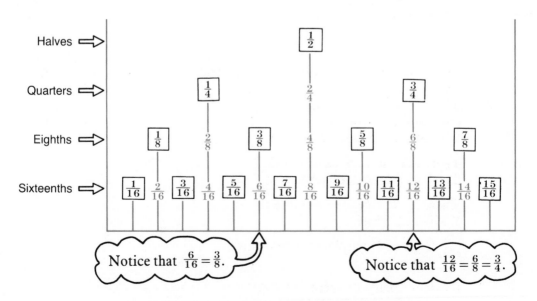

Halves ⇒ $\frac{1}{2}$

Quarters ⇒ $\frac{1}{4}$ $\frac{2}{4}$ $\frac{3}{4}$

Eighths ⇒ $\frac{1}{8}$ $\frac{2}{8}$ $\frac{3}{8}$ $\frac{4}{8}$ $\frac{5}{8}$ $\frac{6}{8}$ $\frac{7}{8}$

Sixteenths ⇒ $\frac{1}{16}$ $\frac{2}{16}$ $\frac{3}{16}$ $\frac{4}{16}$ $\frac{5}{16}$ $\frac{6}{16}$ $\frac{7}{16}$ $\frac{8}{16}$ $\frac{9}{16}$ $\frac{10}{16}$ $\frac{11}{16}$ $\frac{12}{16}$ $\frac{13}{16}$ $\frac{14}{16}$ $\frac{15}{16}$

Notice that $\frac{6}{16} = \frac{3}{8}$.

Notice that $\frac{12}{16} = \frac{6}{8} = \frac{3}{4}$.

The fractions shown in **black** on the diagram are the ones used to name the parts of an inch.

So for example instead of $\frac{10''}{16}$, we would write $\frac{5}{8}''$.

Instead of $\frac{4''}{8}$, we would write $\frac{1}{2}''$.

A1 Write down the length of each line shown below, as a fraction of an inch. (Try to do them without looking at the diagram on the opposite page.)

(a)   (b)   (c)

(d)   (e)   (f)

If you do not have a diagram like the one on the opposite page, you can still change sixteenths to eighths, and so on.

You divide the top and bottom of the fraction by 2, like this:

$$\frac{10}{16} = \frac{5}{8}$$

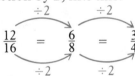

$$\frac{12}{16} = \frac{6}{8} = \frac{3}{4}$$

When you cannot go any further, the fraction is then in its **simplest form** (or its **lowest terms**).

A2 Re-write each of these fractions in its simplest form.
Do them without looking at the diagram on the opposite page.
(a) $\frac{4}{8}$ (b) $\frac{4}{16}$ (c) $\frac{6}{16}$ (d) $\frac{12}{16}$ (e) $\frac{2}{8}$

It is often useful to be able to go the other way, and change halves, quarters and eighths into sixteenths.

To do this you multiply the top and bottom by 2, until you get sixteenths.

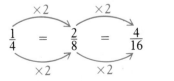

$$\frac{1}{4} = \frac{2}{8} = \frac{4}{16}$$

$$\frac{3}{8} = \frac{6}{16}$$

A3 Change each of these fractions into sixteenths.
(a) $\frac{3}{4}$ (b) $\frac{5}{8}$ (c) $\frac{1}{2}$ (d) $\frac{7}{8}$

A4	Sally wants to tighten a nut on her bike.	A $\frac{1}{4}''$ spanner is too small.	A $\frac{3}{8}''$ spanner is too big.

Sally needs a spanner between $\frac{1}{4}''$ and $\frac{3}{8}''$.

(a) Change $\frac{1}{4}''$ to sixteenths.

(b) Change $\frac{3}{8}''$ to sixteenths.

(c) Write down the size of a spanner which is halfway between $\frac{1}{4}''$ and $\frac{3}{8}''$.

A5 Which of the rods shown below are too big to go through a hole whose diameter is $\frac{5}{8}''$?

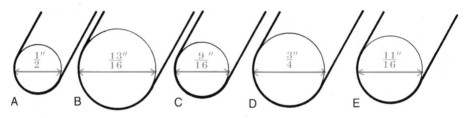

A   B   C   D   E

Adding halves, quarters, eighths and sixteenths

You can easily add halves, quarters, eighths and sixteenths by changing them all to sixteenths (or sometimes eighths).

Worked example

Work out $\frac{3}{8} + \frac{5}{16}$.

Change $\frac{3}{8}$ to sixteenths: $\frac{3}{8} = \frac{6}{16}$.

So $\frac{3}{8} + \frac{5}{16} = \frac{6}{16} + \frac{5}{16} = \frac{11}{16}$.

A6 Work these out.

(a) $\frac{1}{4} + \frac{1}{16}$ (b) $\frac{1}{2} + \frac{5}{16}$ (c) $\frac{5}{8} + \frac{3}{16}$ (d) $\frac{1}{4} + \frac{3}{8}$

(e) $\frac{7}{8} - \frac{1}{16}$ (Subtract!)   (f) $\frac{5}{8} - \frac{3}{16}$ (g) $\frac{1}{2} - \frac{3}{8}$

1 inch is equal to 25·4 millimetres.
We can change fractions of an inch to millimetres, as shown in
the next example.

Worked example

Change $\frac{5}{16}''$ to millimetres, to the nearest millimetre.

1 inch = 25·4 mm

So $\frac{1}{16}$ inch = $\dfrac{25·4}{16}$ mm = 1·5875 mm. Leave this in the calculator display.

So $\frac{5}{16}$ inch = 1·5875 × 5 = 7·9375 mm
$\qquad\qquad\qquad = $ **8 mm** (to the nearest mm).

A7 Change these to millimetres (to the nearest mm).

(a) $\frac{3}{4}''$ (b) $\frac{7}{8}''$ (c) $\frac{11}{16}''$ (d) $\frac{3}{16}''$ (e) $\frac{15}{16}''$

B Writing a fraction in its simplest form

Worked example

There are 48 children at a village school. During a flu epidemic, 30 of
the children were absent.
What fraction of the children were absent? Write the fraction in its
simplest form.

30 out of 48 were absent. As a fraction this is $\frac{30}{48}$.

30 and 48 can both be divided by 2.   Now 15 and 24 can both be divided by 3.

$$\frac{30}{48} \;\overset{\div 2}{=}\; \frac{15}{24} \;\overset{\div 3}{=}\; \frac{5}{8}$$

This is as far as we can go.

The simplest form of the fraction is $\frac{5}{8}$.

(We could also get from $\frac{30}{48}$ to $\frac{5}{8}$ in one step, by dividing top and bottom by 6.)

B1 Write each of these fractions in its simplest form.

(a) $\frac{10}{15}$ (b) $\frac{12}{20}$ (c) $\frac{32}{40}$ (d) $\frac{27}{36}$ (e) $\frac{24}{60}$ (f) $\frac{48}{72}$

B2 A zoo has 20 male monkeys and 12 female monkeys. What fraction
of the monkeys are male? Write the fraction in its simplest form.

Money matters : Borrowing

Suppose you want to buy something expensive. You may decide to borrow the money from a bank. The bank will charge you interest on the amount you borrow, until you repay it.

A simple kind of loan is one which is made for a fixed period, and where the borrower repays the full amount (including interest) at the end of the period.

For example, Anar borrows £500 on 1st June 1987.
The annual interest rate (or APR) is 20%.
Anar agrees to repay the full amount after 3 years, that is on 1st June 1990.

The statement of her account shows how much she owes the bank.

	£	
1st June 87	500·00	
Interest 87–88	+ 100·00	← The first year's interest is 20% of £500.
1st June 88	600·00	← At the end of the first year, she owes £600.
Interest 88–89	+ 120·00	← The second year's interest is 20% of £600.
1st June 89	720·00	← At the end of the second year, she owes £720.
Interest 89–90	+ 144·00	← The third year's interest is 20% of £720.
1st June 90	864·00	← At the end of the third year, she owes £864.
Repayment	− 864·00	← Anar repays £864 on 1st June 1990, . . .
	0	← . . . and cancels the debt.

A much more common way to repay a loan is **instalments**.
The borrower agrees to pay back a certain amount at regular intervals until the loan is repaid.

The bank charges interest on the amount of the loan which is still not repaid. So as the borrower repays, the amounts of interest get smaller and smaller.

For example, John borrows £200 on 1st October 1987. The APR is 15%. John agrees to pay back £60 at the end of each year until the debt is cancelled.

John's statement starts like this:

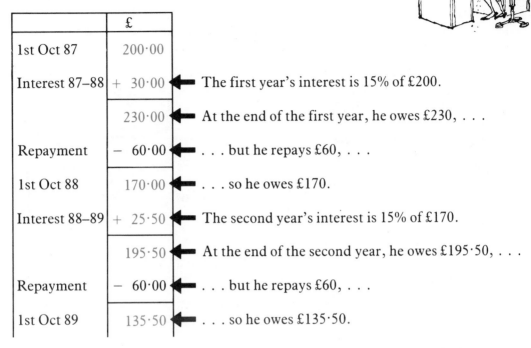

	£
1st Oct 87	200·00
Interest 87–88	+ 30·00 ← The first year's interest is 15% of £200.
	230·00 ← At the end of the first year, he owes £230, . . .
Repayment	− 60·00 ← . . . but he repays £60, . . .
1st Oct 88	170·00 ← . . . so he owes £170.
Interest 88–89	+ 25·50 ← The second year's interest is 15% of £170.
	195·50 ← At the end of the second year, he owes £195·50, . . .
Repayment	− 60·00 ← . . . but he repays £60, . . .
1st Oct 89	135·50 ← . . . so he owes £135·50.

And so on, until the debt is cancelled.

1 Continue the statement above until John's debt is cancelled.
   (The last repayment is less than £60.)

When people buy things on **hire purchase** (HP), they are being given a loan by a hire purchase company. The repayments are usually monthly and they are calculated so that the loan is repaid in an agreed time, for example two years.

The table below gives the sizes of monthly repayments when £100 is borrowed at various different rates of interest.

Time to full repayment

		1 year	2 years	3 years	4 years	5 years
	20%	£9·19	£5·01	£3·63	£2·96	£2·56
	22%	£9·27	£5·09	£3·72	£3·05	£2·65
APR	24%	£9·35	£5·17	£3·80	£3·13	£2·75
	26%	£9·42	£5·25	£3·89	£3·22	£2·84
	28%	£9·50	£5·33	£3·97	£3·31	£2·93
	30%	£9·58	£5·41	£4·06	£3·40	£3·03

Companies which offer loans, including hire purchase loans, are required by law to state the APR.

It is the APR which tells you whether one loan is more expensive than another. The higher the APR, the more expensive is the loan.

Here for example is the same camera on sale in two different shops. The cash price is the same in each shop, but the two shops offer different hire purchase schemes.

Shop A

Shop B

The loan offered by shop A is cheaper than that offered by shop B, because the APR is less (24% as against 26%).

But if you can only afford £4·67 a month, and not £6·20 a month, then you have to choose the more expensive loan.

Here is the same stereo cassette recorder on sale in two different shops. Once again the cash price is the same in both shops.

Shop C

Shop D

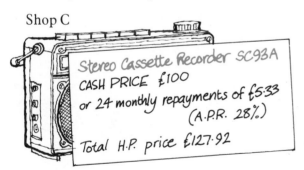

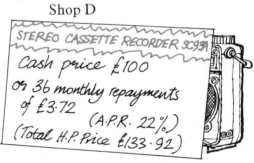

The loan offered by shop D is cheaper than that offered by shop C, because the APR is less (22% as against 28%).

The fact that the 'total HP price' in shop C is less than in shop D is not very important when you want to compare the loans.
Shop D is loaning you money for one year longer than shop C, so you might expect D's 'total price' to be more than C's.

In fact, if shop D were to charge the **same** APR as shop C (28%), the monthly repayments for D would be £3·97 and the 'total price' would be £142·92.

12 Metric units

A Multiplication and division by 10, 100, 1000: a review

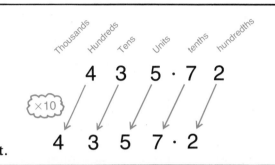

When you multiply a number by **10**,

hundreds become thousands,

tens become hundreds,

units (ones) become tens,

and so on.

Every figure moves **one place to the left**.

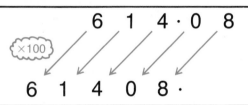

Multiplying by **100** moves every figure **two places to the left**.

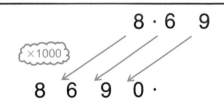

Multiplying by **1000** moves every figure **three places to the left**.

Do not use a calculator for questions A1 to A9.

A1 Multiply each of these numbers by 10.

    (a) 6·8   (b) 0·72   (c) 0·859   (d) 12·74   (e) 0·081

A2 Multiply each of these numbers by 100.

    (a) 3·46   (b) 23·251   (c) 8·7   (d) 16·08   (e) 43·7

A3 Multiply each of these numbers by 1000.

    (a) 1·408   (b) 12·632   (c) 0·8375   (d) 8·005   (e) 0·062

A4 Work out   (a) 0·684 × 100   (b) 7·35 × 10   (c) 0·0054 × 1000

                (d) 100 × 2·007   (e) 1000 × 0·42   (f) 10 × 0·0732

                (g) 6·09 × 1000   (h) 23·2 × 100   (i) 0·083 × 1000

When you divide by 10, every figure moves **one** place to the right.

68·2 ÷10 6·82

When you divide by 100, every figure moves **two** places to the right.

41·7 ÷100 0·417

When you divide by 1000, every figure moves **three** places to the right.

62·8 ÷1000 0·0628

A5 Divide each of these numbers by 10.

(a) 57 (b) 5·7 (c) 6·28 (d) 11·5 (e) 9·06

A6 Divide each of these numbers by 100.

(a) 384 (b) 1635 (c) 69·6 (d) 8·5 (e) 305·8

A7 Divide each of these numbers by 1000.

(a) 6842 (b) 375 (c) 16·3 (d) 148·1 (e) 7·2

A8 Work out (a) 63·4 ÷ 10 (b) 63·4 ÷ 100 (c) 63·4 ÷ 1000
(d) 80·7 ÷ 100 (e) 2·6 ÷ 10 (f) 483 ÷ 1000
(g) 76·2 ÷ 10 (h) 9840 ÷ 1000 (i) 3·72 ÷ 100

A9 Work out (a) 0·86 × 100 (b) 73·2 ÷ 100 (c) 0·48 × 1000
(d) 68·25 ÷ 10 (e) 0·068 × 10 (f) 312·4 ÷ 1000
(g) 183·5 ÷ 100 (h) 6·05 ÷ 10 (i) 0·71 × 1000

B Units of length

Millimetres and centimetres

There are 10 millimetres in 1 centimetre.

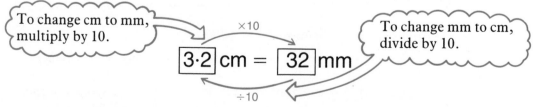

To change cm to mm, multiply by 10.   ×10   3·2 cm = 32 mm   To change mm to cm, divide by 10.   ÷10

B1 Change to mm (a) 16 cm (b) 0·8 cm (c) 5·3 cm (d) 1·85 cm

B2 Change to cm (a) 26 mm (b) 5 mm (c) 315 mm (d) 72 mm

Centimetres and metres

There are 100 cm in 1 metre.

This diagram shows how to change metres to centimetres, and vice versa.

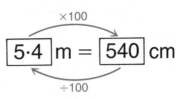

$\times 100$

$5\cdot4 \text{ m} = 540 \text{ cm}$

$\div 100$

B3 Change to cm (a) $1\cdot6$ m (b) $1\cdot67$ m (c) $25\cdot82$ m (d) $0\cdot09$ m

B4 Change to m (a) 183 cm (b) 56 cm (c) 7 cm (d) 1320 cm

B5 Change (a) $3\cdot5$ m to cm (b) $0\cdot8$ cm to mm (c) 3254 cm to m

(d) 32 mm to cm (e) $0\cdot86$ m to cm (f) $18\cdot8$ cm to mm

Metres and kilometres

There are 1000 m in 1 kilometre.

This diagram shows how to change kilometres to metres, and vice versa.

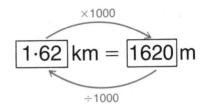

$\times 1000$

$1\cdot62 \text{ km} = 1620 \text{ m}$

$\div 1000$

B6 Change to m (a) 5 km (b) $5\cdot8$ km (c) $0\cdot63$ km (d) $1\cdot862$ km

B7 Change to km (a) 4350 m (b) 232 m (c) 50 m (d) 750 m

B8 Change (a) $63\cdot2$ cm to mm (b) 250 m to km (c) $13\cdot5$ km to m

(d) $0\cdot8$ cm to mm (e) 384 cm to m (f) 27 mm to cm

(g) 65 m to km (h) 82 cm to m (i) 30 m to km

B9 Sadia ran 8 times round a track. The track is 200 m long.
How far did Sadia run, in **kilometres**?

B10 The distance from A to C on this road is $4\cdot2$ km.

From A to B is $3\cdot5$ km.

How far is it from B to C, in **metres**?

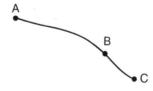

B11 Some workmen are laying a drain, which will be $1\cdot3$ km long.
The drain is made from pipes, each 5 metres long.

(a) Change $1\cdot3$ km to metres.

(b) How many 5-metre pipes will be needed to make the drain?

B12 How many 20 cm lengths of model railway track are needed to
make a total length of $1\cdot8$ metres?

c Units of volume and weight

Millilitres and litres

There are 1000 millilitres in 1 litre.

This diagram shows how to change litres to millilitres, and vice versa.

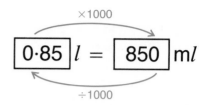

C1 Change to ml   (a) 3 litres   (b) 3·2 litres   (c) 0·8 litre   (d) 0·882 litre

C2 Change to litres   (a) 600 ml   (b) 842 ml   (c) 73 ml   (d) 9 ml

C3 (a) Change 450 ml to litres.   (b) Change 2·3 litres to ml.

    (c) Change 0·06 litre to ml.   (d) Change 48 ml to litres.

A millilitre is the same as $1\,cm^3$.
So there are $1000\,cm^3$ in a litre.

C4 (a) Change $1356\,cm^3$ to litres.   (b) Change 0·88 litre to cm^3.

    (b) Change $420\,cm^3$ to litres.   (c) Change 0·051 litre to cm^3.

Grams and kilograms

There are 1000 grams in 1 kilogram.

This diagram shows how to change kilograms to grams, and vice versa.

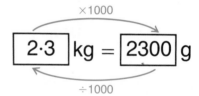

C5 Change to g   (a) 8 kg   (b) 0·65 kg   (c) 4·2 kg   (d) 0·9 kg

C6 Change to kg   (a) 382 g   (b) 56 g   (c) 80 g   (d) 1350 g

C7 Change   (a) 2·5 kg to g   (b) 750 g to kg   (c) 0·66 kg to g

    (d) 1·502 kg to g (e) 1800 g to kg   (f) 20 g to kg

C8 (a) Change 400 ml to litres.   (b) Change 6·2 kg to g.

    (c) Change 8·2 litres to ml.   (d) Change 180 g to kg.

    (e) Change 0·07 kg to g.   (f) Change 1·05 litres to ml.

    (g) Change 3750 ml to litres.   (h) Change 125 g to kg.

C9 (a) How many grams are there in   (i) $\frac{1}{2}$ kg   (ii) $\frac{1}{4}$ kg   (iii) $\frac{3}{4}$ kg

    (b) How many millilitres are there in   (i) $\frac{1}{2}$ litre   (ii) $\frac{1}{4}$ litre   (iii) $\frac{3}{4}$ litre

    (c) How many 250 g packs of butter are needed to make a total weight of 3·5 kg?

D Mixed questions

In many calculations you need to use the same units throughout.
This may mean changing some of the units you are given.

Worked example

A small bottle will hold 80 ml of liquid.
How many of these bottles can be filled from a container holding 1·2 litres?

First change the 1·2 litres into ml.   1·2 litres $= 1·2 \times 1000$ ml
                                                    $= 1200$ ml

Now we have to divide 1200 by 80. $\frac{1200}{80} = 15$

So **15 bottles** can be filled.

D1 How many 150 ml bottles can be filled from 6 litres of liquid?

D2 How many 40 g portions of cheese can be made from 2 kg of cheese?

D3 How many 16 cm lengths of wire can be cut from 20 metres?

D4 80 identical sheets of plastic have a total thickness of 120 cm.
How thick is each sheet, in mm?

D5 A 1p coin has a diameter of 2 cm.

(a) How many 1p coins placed edge to
edge in a line will be needed to make
a total length of 1 metre?

(b) How many will be needed to make
a total length of 1 km?

(c) How much, in £, will 1 km of 1p coins be worth?

D6 A £1 coin is 3 mm thick.

(a) How high, in centimetres, will be a pile containing £50 worth
of £1 coins?

(b) How high, in metres, will be a pile containing £1000 worth
of £1 coins?

D7 The tape in an ordinary cassette player runs past the pick-up
head at a speed of 4·8 cm per second.

Suppose it takes 30 minutes for the whole tape to run past the
pick-up head. How long is the tape, in metres?

13 Formulas and graphs

A The language of algebra: a review

Multiplication

The multiplication sign $\times$ is not used in algebra. It is just left out.

$3a$ means $3 \times a$ pq means $p \times q$ $4xy$ means $4 \times x \times y$.

A1 If $a = 4$, $b = 5$, $c = 2$ and $d = 3$, calculate each of these.

(a) ab (b) $2d$ (c) cd (d) bcd (e) $8bc$ (f) $abcd$

In the expression $ab + cd + ef$, the multiplications $a \times b$, $c \times d$ and $e \times f$ are done first. Then the three results are added together.

For example, suppose $a = 3$, $b = 5$, $c = 4$, $d = 6$, $e = 7$ and $f = 1$. Then

$$
\begin{aligned}
& ab \quad + \quad cd \quad + \quad ef \\
&= (3 \times 5) + (4 \times 6) + (7 \times 1) \\
&= \quad 15 \quad + \quad 24 \quad + \quad 7 \\
&= \quad 46.
\end{aligned}
$$

> When you replace the letters by numbers, you use brackets to show what is done first.

A2 If $w = 3$, $x = 5$, $y = 2$ and $z = 4$, calculate each of these.

(a) $wx + yz$ (b) $wy + xz$ (c) $wz + xy$ (d) $wx - yz$

(e) $w + xy$ (f) $xz - y$ (g) $wz - x - y$ (h) $x + y + 2xy$

Squaring

The squaring symbol ^{2} squares **only** the number or letter it is written against.

$3 + 4^2$ means $3 + (4 \times 4)$ 2×5^2 means $2 \times (5 \times 5)$

A3 Calculate each of these.

(a) $2 + 3^2$ (b) $3 + 2^2$ (c) 2×5^2 (d) $20 - 4^2$ (e) 3×10^2

$3a^2$ means $3 \times a^2$. So if $a = 4$, then $3a^2 = 3 \times 4^2$ ('3 times **4-squared**')
$$= 3 \times 16 = 48.$$

A4 If $p = 5$, $q = 2$, $r = 3$ and $s = 6$, calculate each of these.

(a) $2p^2$ (b) $3q^2$ (c) $p - q^2$ (d) $ps + r^2$ (e) $ps - r^2$

(f) pq^2 (g) qp^2 (h) pqr^2 (i) $p + 2r^2$ (j) $pq^2 - rs$

Division

$\frac{a}{b}$ means $a \div b$.

A5 If $a = 8$, $b = 2$, $c = 12$ and $d = 3$, calculate each of these.

(a) $\frac{a}{b}$ (b) $\frac{c}{d}$ (c) $\frac{a}{b} + \frac{c}{d}$ (d) $\frac{ad}{c}$ (e) $a + \frac{c}{b}$ (f) $\frac{a+c}{b}$ (g) $\frac{c}{d-b}$

Brackets

Brackets show what is done first.

$a(b + c)$ means 'a times **b-plus-c**'.

For example, if $a = 3$, $b = 5$ and $c = 2$, then

$$a(b + c)$$
$$= 3 \times \underline{(5 + 2)}$$
$$= 3 \times \quad 7$$
$$= 21$$

The brackets show that we add $5 + 2$ first.

A6 If $w = 5$, $x = 3$, $y = 8$ and $z = 6$, calculate each of these.

(a) $2(w + x)$ (b) $x(y - z)$ (c) $z(y - x)$ (d) $(z - x)^2$ (e) $\frac{z(y - z)}{x}$

A7 If $a = 4$, $b = 7$, $c = 2$ and $d = 3$, calculate each of these.

(a) $a + cd$ (b) $ab + c$ (c) $a(b + c)$ (d) cd^2 (e) $b + \frac{a}{c}$ (f) $\frac{a}{b - d}$

B Substituting numbers into formulas

B1 The diagram on the right shows the end wall of a shed.

f stands for the front height, in m.
b stands for the back height, in m.
w stands for the width, in m.

There is a formula for the area of the wall.
It is

$$A = \frac{w(f + b)}{2}.$$

A stands for the area in m^2. Find A when

(a) $f = 3$, $b = 2$ and $w = 2$ (b) $f = 2 \cdot 5$, $b = 1 \cdot 5$ and $w = 3$
(c) $f = 2 \cdot 4$, $b = 1 \cdot 6$ and $w = 1 \cdot 8$ (d) $f = 2 \cdot 4$, $b = 1 \cdot 8$ and $w = 1 \cdot 4$

B2 The area of an equilateral triangle is given approximately by the formula $A = 0 \cdot 43 s^2$.
A is the area in cm^2, and s is the length of each side in cm.

Calculate A when   (a) $s = 3$ (b) $s = 5$ (c) $s = 6 \cdot 5$

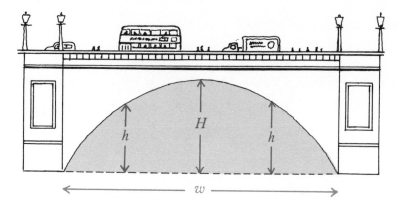

B3 The area of a symmetrical arch shape can be calculated **approximately** from the measurements shown in the diagram.

w is the width of the arch, in metres.
H is the maximum height in m, measured at the middle of the arch.
h is the height measured at either $\frac{1}{4}$ or $\frac{3}{4}$ of the distance across.

The formula which gives the area approximately is

$$A = \frac{w(H + 4h)}{6}.$$

A is the area in m².

Use this formula to find A when

(a) $H = 3$, $h = 2$ and $w = 9$ (b) $H = 10$, $h = 6$ and $w = 24$

(c) $H = 7$, $h = 6{\cdot}5$ and $w = 20$ (d) $H = 4{\cdot}5$, $h = 3$ and $w = 10$

B4 A factory makes saucepans. The inside surface of each saucepan is coated with a 'non-stick' coating.

When a new size of saucepan is made, the manufacturers need to work out the area of the inside surface, to see how much non-stick coating will be needed.

Here is the formula for working out the area of the inside surface.

$$S = \pi D\left(\frac{D}{4} + d\right).$$

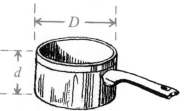

D is the diameter of the saucepan, in cm.
d is the depth of the saucepan, in cm.
S is the inside surface area, in cm².
π, as usual, has the value $3{\cdot}14\ldots$

(a) Use the formula to calculate S when $D = 20$ and $d = 13$.
    (Work out the value of $\frac{D}{4} + d$ first, then do $\pi \times D \times \left(\frac{D}{4} + d\right)$.

(b) Calculate S when   (i) $D = 24$ and $d = 17$ (ii) $D = 18$ and $d = 10$

c Graphs from formulas

When the driver of a car suddenly puts her foot on the brake, the
car does not stop immediately. It takes a little time to come to
a stop, and during this time the car moves forward a certain
distance.

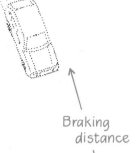

The distance moved depends on how fast the car is travelling
when the brakes are applied. If the speed of the car is S m.p.h.,
the braking distance B, in metres, is given by this formula:

Braking
distance

$$B = \frac{S^2}{60}.$$

The relationship between speed, S, and braking distance, B, can be
shown in a graph.

There are two stages in drawing the graph.

1 We use the formula to make a table of values of S and B.

For example, we calculate B when
S is 0, 10, 20, 30, . . .

If $S=0$, then $B = \dfrac{0^2}{60} = 0$

If $S=10$, then $B = \dfrac{10^2}{60} = \dfrac{100}{60} = 1\cdot7$ (to 1 d.p.)

and so on

. . . and we make a table of the results.

S (speed in m.p.h.)	0	10	20	30 . . .
B (braking distance in m)	0	1·7	6·7	15·0 . . .

2 We choose suitable scales for the axes
(S across and B up).

We plot the points from the table, and
draw a smooth curve through them.

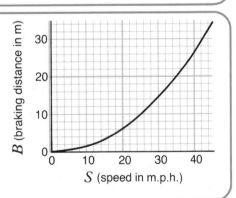

C1 (a) Copy the table of values above, and continue it for values of S up to 70.

(b) Draw the graph for values of S up to 70.

(c) Use your graph to find B when S is 35, and check by calculation.

(d) Use your graph to find the speed for which the braking distance is 50 m.

C2 Suppose a driver sees a child run out into the road ahead. It takes a little time to think before applying the brakes, and during this time the car travels forward. Then the brakes are applied and the car travels a bit further as it slows down to a stop.

The total distance travelled between the driver seeing the child and the car stopping is called the 'stopping distance'. It can be calculated from this formula:

$$D = \frac{S(S + 20)}{60}.$$

S is the speed of the car, in m.p.h., before the brakes are applied.
D is the stopping distance, in metres.

(a) Copy and complete this calculation to find the value of D when S is 10.

$$D = \frac{10(10 + 20)}{60}$$
$$= \frac{10 \times 30}{60} = \frac{300}{60} = \ldots$$

(b) Calculate D when S is 0, 10, 20, 30 . . . up to 70, and make a table of the results, like this. (Give values of D to 1 d.p.)

S (speed in m.p.h.)	0	10	20	30	. . .
D (stopping distance in m)					

(c) Draw a graph with S across and D up.

(d) Use your graph to find the speed for which the stopping distance is 50 m.

C3 A child drops a stone from the top of a cliff which is 80 m above the level of the sea below.

The height of the stone during its fall can be calculated from this formula:
$$h = 80 - 5t^2.$$
t is the time in seconds since the stone was dropped.
h is the height of the stone in metres above sea-level.

(a) Copy and complete this calculation to find h when t is 3.

$$h = 80 - (5 \times 3^2)$$
$$= 80 - (5 \times 9) = \ldots$$

(b) Calculate h when t is 0, 1, 2, 3 and 4. Make a table of the results, like this.

t	0	1	2	3	4
h					

(c) Draw a graph t across and h up.

(d) Does the stone fall at the same speed all the time, or does it speed up or does it slow down?

(e) How many seconds after being dropped is it 40 m above sea-level?

C4 There are two different scales which are commonly used for measuring temperature. One is the Celsius or Centigrade scale, the other is the Fahrenheit scale.

The temperature at which water freezes is 0°C on the Celsius scale, and 32°F on the Fahrenheit scale.

The temperature at which water boils is 100°C on the Celsius scale, and 212°F on the Fahrenheit scale.

There is a formula for changing a temperature from Celsius to Fahrenheit. It is

$$f = 1 \cdot 8c + 32.$$

c stands for the temperature in °C.
f stands for the temperature in °F.

(a) Copy this table and use the formula to complete it.

c	0	10	20	30	40
f					

(b) Draw a graph with c across and f up.

(c) Use the graph to change 60°F to degrees Celsius.

C5 Saraj has to drive a distance of 120 miles.
If she drives at an average speed of S m.p.h., the time taken for the journey is given by the formula

$$T = \frac{120}{S}.$$

T is the journey time in hours.

(a) Calculate T when S is 20, 30, 40, 50 and 60, and write the results in a table.

S	20	30	40	50	60
T					

(b) Draw a graph with S across and T up.

(c) What happens to T as S gets larger and larger?

(d) What happens to T as S gets smaller and smaller?

(e) Why is it impossible to calculate T when S is 0?

9 Squares and square roots

9.1   What number is the square of   (a) 5   (b) 7   (c) 10

9.2   What number is the square root of   (a) 16   (b) 1   (c) 64

9.3   Copy these sentences and fill in the blanks.

(a) ... is the square root of 9.   (b) ... is the square of 9.

(c) 4 is the square of ...   (d) 7 is the square root of ...

10   Arranging and selecting

10.1   Suppose you have three rubber stamps, for printing the figures 1, 2 and 3.

What different three-figure numbers could you print? (A figure can be repeated. For example, 313 is possible.)

How many different three-figure numbers could be printed?

10.2   Highlands College sweatshirts are available in three sizes: small, medium and large. Buyers have a choice of five colours: red, blue, orange, yellow and green.

The college shop stocks all sizes and colours. How many different combinations of size and colour are there?

11   Fractions

11.1   Change these to sixteenths.

(a) $\frac{3}{8}$ (b) $\frac{3}{4}$ (c) $\frac{1}{2}$ (d) $\frac{7}{8}$

11.2   Which fraction is halfway between

(a) $\frac{5}{8}$ and $\frac{3}{4}$ (b) $\frac{3}{4}$ and 1   (c) $\frac{3}{8}$ and $\frac{1}{2}$ (c) $\frac{1}{8}$ and $\frac{1}{4}$

11.3   Write each of these fractions in its simplest form.

(a) $\frac{6}{8}$ (b) $\frac{20}{25}$ (c) $\frac{12}{18}$ (d) $\frac{36}{40}$ (e) $\frac{35}{40}$

12 Metric units

12.1 (a) Change 56 mm to cm. (b) Change 35 cm to m.

(c) Change 3·6 km to m. (d) Change 450 m to km.

(e) Change 950 g to kg. (f) Change 0·07 litre to ml.

12.2 How many 80 g portions of cheese can be cut from 1·2 kg of cheese?

12.3 How many 30 cm pieces of wire can be cut from a 60-metre roll of wire?

13 Formulas and graphs

13.1 If $a = 5$, $b = 3$, $c = 2$, and $d = 6$, calculate each of these.

(a) $ab + c$ (b) $a(b + c)$ (c) $a^2 + b^2$ (d) $2a^2$ (e) $3c^2$

(f) $\dfrac{d}{c} - b$ (g) $\dfrac{a + b}{c}$ (h) $\dfrac{d}{a - c}$ (i) $a + \dfrac{b}{c}$ (j) $\dfrac{cd}{a - b}$

13.2 The depth of a well can be found by dropping a stone into it and measuring the time taken for the stone to reach the bottom.

The depth, d metres, can be calculated approximately from the formula

$$d = 5t^2$$

where t is the time taken, in seconds, for a stone to reach the bottom.

(a) Use the formula to calculate d when $t = 0, 1, 2, 3, 4$ and 5. Write your results in a table.

t	0	1	2	3	4	5
d						

(b) Draw axes with t across and d up. Use the scales shown here.

Plot the points from the table and draw a smooth curve throught them.

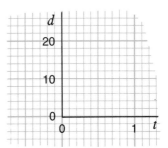

(c) Use the graph to find

(i) the depth of a well where a stone takes 2·6 seconds to reach the bottom

(ii) the time taken for a stone to reach the bottom of a well 50 m deep

Whole numbers and decimals

1.1 How many bottles of salad cream are there in 12 boxes like this one?

1.2 At the start of a week there were 354 tins of baked beans in a supermarket. At the end of the week there were 78 left. How many tins were sold?

1.3 During one week on a rabbit farm, 130 new rabbits were born and 45 old ones died. At the end of the week there were 850 rabbits altogether. How many were there at the start of that week?

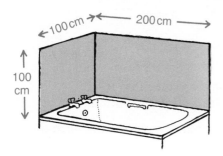

1.4 The shaded part of the wall in this picture is to be covered by tiles.
Each tile is a square 10 cm by 10 cm.

How many tiles will be needed?

1.5 Jars of jam are packed into cardboard boxes. Each box holds 100 jars. There are 3685 jars to be packed.
(a) How many boxes can be filled?
(b) How many jars will be left over?

1.6 Without using a calculator, say which of these you could buy with a £20 note.
(a) 38 metres of hosepipe at 47p per metre
(b) 4·5 metres of curtain fabric at £5·25 per metre
(c) 120 metres of nylon rope at 21p per metre

1.7 When Brenda puts her gas fire on 'high', the gas it uses costs 68p per hour. How much does it cost to have it on 'high'
(a) for 8 hours   (b) for $2\frac{1}{4}$ hours
(c) over the weekend, from 6 p.m. Friday to 8 a.m. Monday

1.8 Calculate these costs to the nearest thousand pounds.
(a) The cost of educating 225 children at £3260 each per year
(b) The cost of feeding 225 children at £970 each per year
(c) The cost of clothing 225 children at £125 each per year

1.9 (a) 6 people share a 5 kg sack of potatoes. What weight does each get?
  (b) 5 people share a 6 kg sack. What weight does each get?

1.10 A station buffet sells coffee in standard cups (240 ml) at 38p, or in large beakers (330 ml) at 55p. Which is better value?

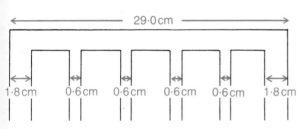

1.11 This picture shows a sheet of stick-on labels. Each label is 2·5 cm wide and 1·5 cm high. The sheet is 65 cm wide and 48 cm high.

How many labels are there on the sheet?

1.12 A bottle contains 0·6 litre of cough mixture. The 'adult dose' is three medicine spoonfuls. A medicine spoon holds 5 ml.

How many adult doses can you get from the bottle?

1.13 This diagram shows a page in a newspaper. All five columns are the same width.

How wide is each column?

1.14 Write these numbers in order of size, largest first.
  6·08   4·289   0·367   6·3   0·0295   1·7   0·009 88

1.15 Round off (a) 25 930 to the nearest thousand   (b) 35·7876 to 2 d.p.
           (c) 0·0478 to 2 d.p.   (d) 7·4397 to 2 d.p.

1.16 The population of Bristol is 401 100. The population of Reading is 137 000. Copy and complete this sentence:

The population of Bristol is about . . . times that of Reading.

1.17 The entrance fee to an exhibition is 65p. During one day £119·60 was taken at the door. How many people paid to see the exhibition?

1.18 17 students and 2 teachers are going on a trip abroad. The cost is £88 per person, but one teacher is allowed to go free. All the people who are going agree to share the total cost of the trip equally between them. How much does each person pay?

2 Percentage

2.1 Re-write these statements using percentages.

(a)
I'll tell you what, I'll reduce the price by a quarter.

(b)
7 out of 10 students finish the course.

(c)
$\frac{2}{5}$ of government expenditure goes on education.

2.2 Calculate (a) 45% of £80 (b) 8% of £24·50 (c) 13% of £550

2.3 A farmer had 74 cows. 48 of them caught a disease. What percentage of the cows caught the disease? (Give it to the nearest 1%.)

2.4 What is each of these as a percentage (to the nearest 1%)?
(a) 86 out of 200 (b) 7 out of 12 (c) 17 out of 230 (d) 9 out of 240

2.5 Gold jewellery is never made from 100% gold because it would be too soft. It is made from an alloy of gold and some other metal such as silver.

The amount of gold in the alloy is measured in 'carats'. The maximum number (for pure gold) is 24 carats. So '12 carat gold' is an alloy which has $\frac{12}{24}$ of its weight pure gold. (In other words, $\frac{1}{2}$ or 50% of the alloy is pure gold.)

(a) What percentage of '18 carat gold' is pure gold?
(b) What percentage of '22 carat gold' is pure gold?
(c) If you made an alloy which was 25% pure gold and 75% other metals, how could you describe it using carats?

2.6 All the people working in a factory get a wage rise of 6%. Stella earns £56·50 a week now. How much will she earn after the increase?

2.7 (a) Increase £85 by 15%. (b) Increase £265 by 45%.

2.8 A boutique has a sale. Handbags are reduced in price by 30%. What is the sale price of a handbag which before the sale cost
(a) £50 (b) £18·50 (c) £6·99 (d) £24·99

2.9 A garage reduces the price of a secondhand car from £1750 to £1625.
(a) How much was taken off the price?
(b) What was the percentage reduction in the price, to the nearest 1%?

2.10 Before a fare increase, Jackie's weekly season ticket cost £11·40. After the increase it went up to £13·60.
(a) What was the percentage increase in the fare, to the nearest 1%?
(b) Carol's fare went up from £8·90 to £11·00. Was this a larger or a smaller percentage increase than Jackie's? Show your working.

3 Unitary method and ratio

3.1 The labour charge for a repair job which took 6 hours was £58·50.
(a) What was the cost of 1 hour's labour?
(b) How much would the charge be for 14 hours?

3.2 It took 8 full truckloads to get rid of 220 cubic metres of earth.
How much earth would be carried in 11 full truckloads?

3.3 100 g of marmalade contains 68 g of sugar.
How much sugar is there in 250 g of marmalade?

3.4 Sheila and Ramesh cleared a site and earned £450 between them.
Sheila worked for 4 days and Ramesh for 3 days, so they agreed
to split the money in the ratio 4 to 3.

How much did each get, to the nearest penny?

3.5 Audrey runs a health food shop. She sells a mixture of peanuts
and raisins. She mixes nuts and raisins in the ratio 3 to 2
by weight.

(a) What weight of nuts does she mix with 5 kg of raisins?

(b) Audrey charges £1·50 a kg for nuts sold separately, and
£2·50 a kg for raisins. What should she charge for 1 kg of the
mixture?

4 Fractions

4.1 Calculate these.

(a) $\frac{3}{4}$ of £84   (b) $\frac{2}{3}$ of £67·20   (c) $\frac{1}{5}$ of £180   (d) $\frac{7}{10}$ of £4·20

4.2 A kilometre is about $\frac{5}{8}$ of a mile.
Use this to change 100 km to miles.

4.3 Change $\frac{5}{16}$ to a decimal.

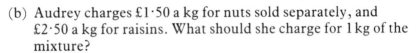

4.4 The sizes of five nuts (in inches) are $\frac{11''}{16}$, $\frac{1''}{2}$, $\frac{5''}{8}$, $\frac{15''}{16}$ and $\frac{3''}{4}$.
Put them in order of size, starting with the smallest.

4.5 You are trying to tighten a bolt. A $\frac{3''}{4}$ spanner is just too small.
A $\frac{7''}{8}$ spanner is just too big. Which size is halfway between the two?

4.6 1 inch is equal to 25·4 mm.
What are these equal to in mm, to the nearest 0·1 mm?

(a) $\frac{1''}{4}$ (b) $\frac{3''}{4}$ (c) $\frac{5''}{8}$ (d) $\frac{13''}{16}$

5 Time

5.1 Write using the 24-hour clock (a) 5:15 p.m. (b) 10:45 p.m. (c) 8:05 p.m.

5.2 Write these times using a.m. or p.m. (a) 1510 (b) 2153 (c) 0620

5.3 This is part of a bus timetable.

High Street	1142 and every 15 minutes until	2012
The Plough	1155	2025
Elm Corner	1209	2039
Park Place	1218	2048

(a) How long does a bus take to travel from High Street to Park Place?

(b) Jason just misses the 1155 bus from The Plough. At what time does the next bus leave?

(c) The last bus of the day leaves High Street at 2012. At what time does the last but one bus leave High Street?

6 Rates

6.1 A plane flies at a steady speed of 500 m.p.h.

(a) How far does it travel in $5\frac{1}{2}$ hours?

(b) How long would it take to fly 4500 miles?

6.2 Calculate the average speed of an aircraft which covered a distance of 820 miles in $2\frac{1}{4}$ hours. Give the speed to the nearest m.p.h.

6.3 Worldwings Airways plan a new service from London to Moscow, a distance of 1880 miles. They plan to use an aircraft which flies at 500 m.p.h. How long will the journey take, to the nearest $\frac{1}{4}$ hour?

6.4 Kate took $2\frac{1}{4}$ minutes to take down 156 words in shorthand. Calculate her rate in words per minute, to the nearest whole number.

6.5 Robert charged £11·00 for typing 17 pages.

(a) What does this work out at in pence per page, to the nearest penny?

(b) How much would he charge at this rate for 44 similar pages?

6.6 If a telephone call abroad costs 5p for 6 seconds, how much will a $3\frac{1}{2}$ minute call cost?

6.7 A ciné film runs through a projector at a rate of 18 frames per second. How many frames are there altogether in a film which lasts for $1\frac{1}{2}$ hours? Round off your answer to the nearest thousand.

7 Negative numbers

7.1 Work out the rise or fall in temperature in each of these. Write each answer like this: '10 degree rise' or '7 degree fall' and so on.

(a) From $^-2°C$ to $^-10°C$ (b) From $6°C$ to $^-5°C$

(c) From $^-12°C$ to $^-3°C$ (d) From $^-8°C$ to $15°C$

7.2 The temperature at midday was $8°C$. It fell by 15 degrees between midday and midnight, and then rose by 9 degrees by dawn. What was the temperature   (a) at midnight   (b) at dawn

8 Formulas

8.1 The volume of a pyramid can be calculated from the formula
$$V = \frac{Ah}{3}.$$

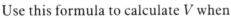

A is the area of the base of the pyramid, in cm^2.
h is the height of the pyramid, in cm.
V is the volume, in cm^3.

Use this formula to calculate V when
(a) $A = 25$ and $h = 9$ (b) $A = 16\cdot8$ and $h = 4\cdot2$

8.2 If $a = 5$, $b = 2$ and $c = 4$, calculate the value of each of these.

(a) $2a^2$ (b) ab^2 (c) abc (d) $ab + c^2$ (e) $a(b + c)$ (f) $\dfrac{a}{c - b}$

8.3 Reference books of medicines and drugs usually give the size of an adult dose of each drug. One of the rules used by nurses to work out children's doses is called 'Young's rule'. It is
$$C = \frac{An}{n + 12}.$$

C stands for the child's dose, A for the adult's dose, and n for the child's age in years. (The rule is not used for babies less than 1 year old.)

(a) Use the rule to calculate the dose for an 8 year old child when the adult dose is 15 milligrams (mg).
(b) A rule used to calculate the dose for a child less than 1 year old is called 'Fried's rule'. It is
$$C = \frac{Am}{150}.$$

m is the child's age in months.
Calculate the dose for a 9 month old child when the adult dose is 400 mg.

8.4 The weight in kg that can be supported at the middle of an oak beam is given by the formula
$$w = \frac{60\,bd^2}{l}.$$
w stands for the weight in kg, and b, d and l for the breadth, depth and length of the beam in cm.
Calculate the load which can be supported by an oak beam 400 cm long, 20 cm broad and 32 cm deep.

9 Graphs

9.1 An oven is switched on. The temperature rises slowly at first, then faster, and then more slowly again until it reaches a maximum. Then it stays constant. Sketch a graphy to show all this.

9.2 This is the graph of a coach journey from London to Birmingham (110 miles).

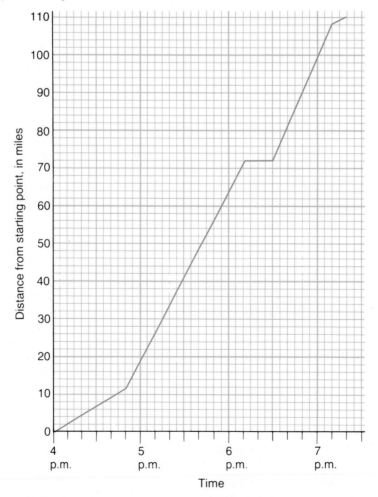

(a) The coach left a coach station in London at 4 p.m. It drove to the start of the motorway. How long did it take to reach the motorway?

(b) How far was it from the coach station to the motorway?

(c) Why is the graph flat between 6:10 p.m. and 6:30 p.m.? What do you think was happening then?

(d) Why do you think the last part of the graph is less steep?

9.3 An object is thrown vertically upwards. The height it reaches depends on the speed at which it is thrown. The formula for the height is

$h = \dfrac{u^2}{10}$. (h is the height in m; u is the speed of throwing, in m/s.)

(a) Copy and complete this table.

u	0	10	20	30	40	50
h						

(b) Draw a graph with u across (1 cm to 10 m/s) and h up (1 cm to 50 m). Use it to find u when h is 120.

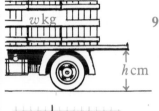

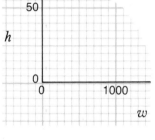

9.4 The height of the platform of this lorry above the road level depends on the weight on the platform.

The formula for the height is $h = 180 - \dfrac{w}{50}$.

h is the height in cm; w is the weight in kilograms.

(a) Calculate h when w is 0, 1000, 2000, etc. up to 5000. Write the results in a table.

(b) Draw a graph, with w across and h up. Use the scales shown on the left.

(c) The minimum safe value for h is 110. Use the graph to find the maximum load which can be put on the platform.

10 Coordinates

10.1 Copy this diagram.

(a) Mark the points A ($^-2$, 1), B (3, 0) and C (3, 2).

Join them up to make a triangle.

(b) What is special about this triangle?

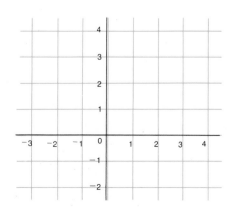

10.2 Copy this diagram.

(a) Write down the coordinates of C.

(b) A, B and C are three of the corner points of a rectangle. The fourth corner is at a point D. Mark the point D on the diagram.

(c) Write down the coordinates of D.

(d) Draw the two diagonals of the rectangle ABCD. Write down the coordinates of the point where they cross.

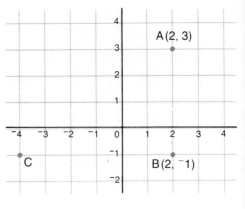

10.3 Copy this diagram.

(a) Write down the coordinates of P, Q and R.

(b) P, Q and R are three of the four corner points of a square. The fourth corner is at a point S.

Mark S on the diagram and draw the square PQRS.

(c) Write down the coordinates of S.

(d) Write down the coordinates of the centre point of the square.

(e) What is the angle between the lines PQ and PR?

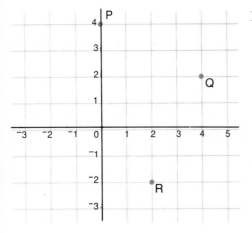

10.4 Copy this diagram.

(a) The dotted line is a mirror line. Reflect the triangle ABC in the mirror line. Draw the image triangle and letter it A′, B′, C′.

(b) Write down the coordinates of A′, B′ and C′.

11 Area and perimeter

11.1 Calculate the area of

(a) a rectangle 24 m by 15 m   (b) a square of side 25 m

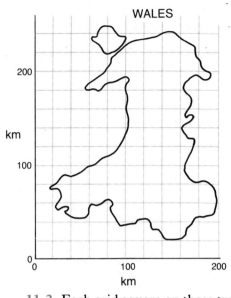

WALES

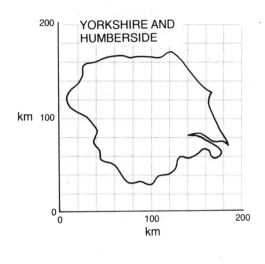

YORKSHIRE AND HUMBERSIDE

11.2 Each grid square on these two maps represents a square 20 km by 20 km.

(a) What area does each grid square represent?

(b) Estimate the area of (i) Wales (ii) Yorkshire and Humberside
(Do not mark the maps. You can trace them if you like.)

(c) At the 1981 census, the population of Wales was 2 790 000,
and that of Yorkshire and Humberside 4 840 000.
Roughly how many people were there on average for each square
kilometre in (i) Wales (ii) Yorkshire and Humberside

11.3 Calculate the perimeter of

(a) a triangle, with sides of length 10 m, 15 m and 23 m

(b) a rectangle 30 m by 10 m   (c) a square of side 8 m

11.4 Calculate the area of
each of these triangles.

(a)

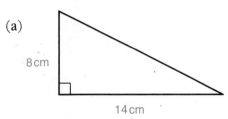

8 cm

14 cm

(b)

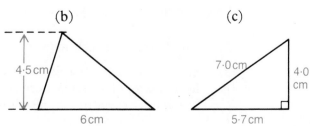

4·5 cm

6 cm

(c)

7·0 cm

4·0 cm

5·7 cm

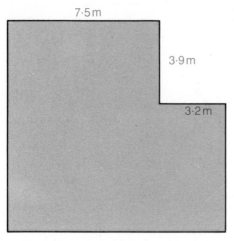

7·5m

3·9m

3·2m

6·8m

11.5 This is the floor plan of a room.
All the angles are right-angles.

(a) A sealing strip is to be laid round
the perimeter of the floor.
Calculate the total length of
the strip.

(b) Calculate the area of the floor.
(You may find it helpful to draw your
own sketch of the plan, and divide
it up to find the area.)

(c) Round off the area to the nearest m^2.

(d) The floor has to be varnished.
1 litre of varnish will cover about
4·5 m^2 of the floor. Roughly how many
litres will be needed?

12 The circle

12.1

20 cm wide

You can buy a 'jacket' to fit round
a hot water tank. It is made up of
'panels' like the one on the right.

(a) About how many panels 20 cm wide would you need to go round
a tank of diameter 42 cm? (Overestimate rather than underestimate.)

(b) About how many do you need to go round a tank 55 cm in diameter?

12.2 This label . . .   . . . fits round this tin without overlap.

CAT
FOOD

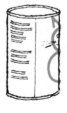

7·5cm

Calculate the length of the label to the nearest 0·1 cm.

12.3 Calculate these. Give each answer to the nearest 0·1 cm.

(a) The circumference of a circle of diameter 12·8 cm
(b) The diameter of a circle whose circumference is 76·8 cm
(c) The circumference of a circle whose radius is 8·8 cm

13 Angles

13.1 Measure the angles marked *a*, *b*, *c* and *d*.

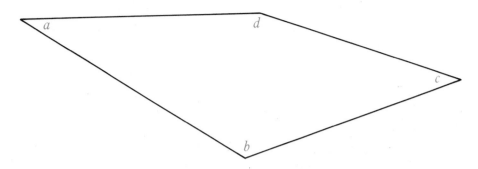

13.2 Calculate the angles marked with letters in each of these diagrams.
(Do not try to measure them; they are not drawn accurately.)

(a)   (b)   (c)

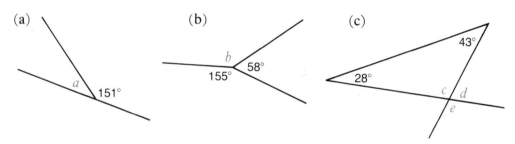

13.3 This map shows some islands
A helicopter takes off from X.
Which islands does it fly over
if it flies on a bearing of

(a) 060° (b) 140° (c) 255° (d) 295°

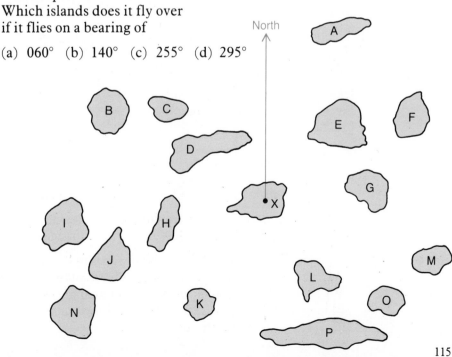

14 Scale drawing

14.1 The sketch on the right shows a greenhouse, and a cold frame standing next to it.

The sketch below shows the end of the greenhouse and cold frame. Measurements are in cm.

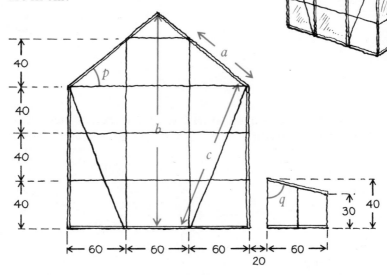

(a) Using a scale of 1 cm to 20 cm, make a scale drawing of the end of the greenhouse and cold frame.

(b) From the scale drawing, measure the lengths *a*, *b* and *c*.

(c) Measure the angles *p* and *q*.

(d) The lid of the cold frame is hinged. When it is open, it rests against the side wall of the greenhouse.

Use your scale drawing to find how far up the side of the greenhouse it touches.

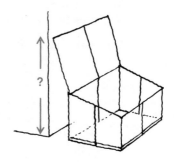

14.2 This is a rough sketch of a triangular piece of land.

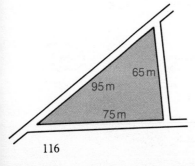

(a) Make a scale drawing of the triangle. Use a scale of 1 cm to 10 m. Describe how you made your drawing.

(b) The owner of the land wants to know if there is room to build a prefabricated barn on the piece of land. The plan of the barn is a rectangle 40 m by 35 m. Draw the rectangle to scale on tracing paper and see if it will fit into the triangle.

15 Maps

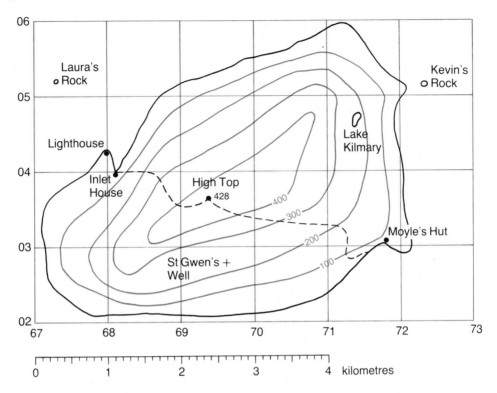

This is a map of an island.

15.1 (a) What is the four-figure grid reference of the square which Lake Kilmary is in?

(b) What is the six-figure grid reference of each of these?
  (i) Inlet House   (ii) High Top   (iii) Moyle's Hut
  (iv) Laura's Rock   (v) St Gwen's Well   (vi) Kevin's Rock

15.2 The height of St Gwen's Well above sea-level is between 200 m and 300 m. Find each of the points whose grid references are given below, and write the height at that point in the form 'between . . . and . . .'.
(a) 675032   (b) 683027   (c) 715036   (d) 695053   (e) 717040

15.3 There are two paths to High Top marked on the map. Which is steeper, the path from Inlet House or the path from Moyle's Hut? How can you tell?

15.4 Find the two points on the coast which are furthest apart and find the distance between them in km.

15.5 At low tide it is possible to walk all round the coastline of the island. Estimate the distance all round the island.

16 Symmetry

16.1   Copy this drawing of a regular hexagon.
       Mark all of its lines of reflection symmetry.

16.2   (a) Draw a triangle with only one line of reflection symmetry.

       (b) Draw a quadrilateral with only one line of reflection symmetry.

16.3   Copy these as accurately as you can.
       Mark any lines of reflection symmetry as dotted lines. ---

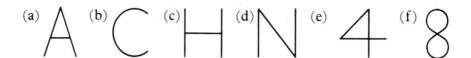

(a) A   (b) C   (c) H   (d) N   (e) 4   (f) 8

16.4   If you reflect design A in the dotted
       line, which of those below will you see?

16.5   Copy each of these diagrams.
       Complete each design by reflecting in the the dotted line.

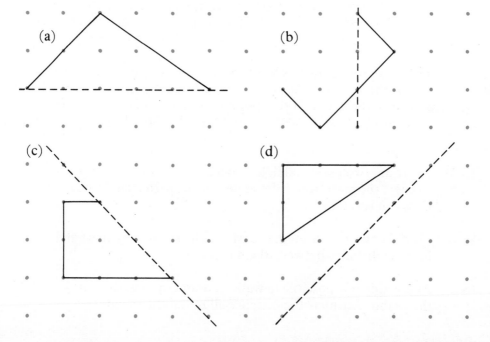

(a)

(b)

(c)

(d)

17 Three dimensions

17.1 A child's toy consists of a solid block of wood with four wheels. Here are a side elevation and a front elevation of the toy, drawn to a scale of 1 cm to 10 cm.

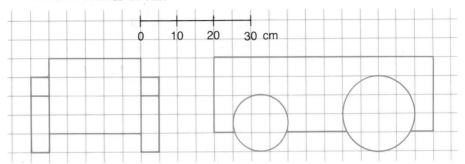

Draw, to the same scale, a plan view of the toy.

17.2 This is a plan view of a house.

The pictures below are pictures of the house. From what direction (north, north-east, etc.) was each picture taken?

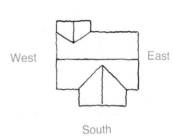

North

West   East

South

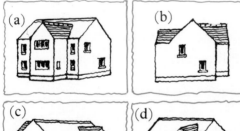

(a)

(b)

(c)

(d)

(e)

17.3 (a) Draw, full-size, a net for the solid shown on the right.

(b) Sketch the solid whose net is shown below. (Tabs for sticking are not shown.)

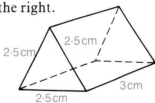

2·5 cm

2·5 cm

2·5 cm

3 cm

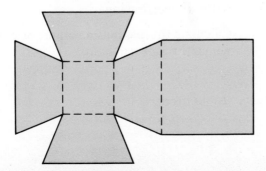

18 Metric units

18.1   (a) Change 3420 m to km.   (b) Change 652 mm to cm.

        (c) Change 759 m to km.   (d) Change 1060 cm to m.

18.2   (a) Change 350 g to kg.   (b) Change 0·6 kg to g.

        (c) Change 1080 g to kg.   (d) Change 4·2 kg to g.

18.3   (a) Change 362 ml to litres.   (b) Change 0·65 litre to ml.

        (c) Change 25 ml to litres.   (d) Change 5·02 litres to ml.

18.4   How many 5 ml measures of medicine can be poured from 1 litre?

18.5   How many 40 cm lengths of wire can be cut from 12 metres?

18.6   80 sheets of plywood, each 7 mm thick, are piled on top of one another. Calculate the height of the pile, in **centimetres**.

18.7   500 sheets of typing paper have a total weight of 2·5 kg. How much does each sheet weigh, in **grams**?

19 Volume

Reminder.   1 cm³ is equal to 1 millilitre (ml).   1 litre = 1000 ml = 1000 cm³.

19.1   (a) Calculate the volume of this block, to the nearest 0·1 cm³.

        (b) What would the block weigh if it was made of metal weighing 8·5 grams per cm³? Give the weight to the nearest gram.

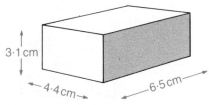

        (c) What would the block weigh if it was made of plastic weighing 0·85 grams per cm³?

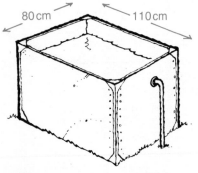

19.2   This water tank can be filled to a depth of 65 cm without overflowing.

Calculate the maximum volume of water which the tank can hold

(a) in cm³

(b) in litres

20 Enlargement and reduction

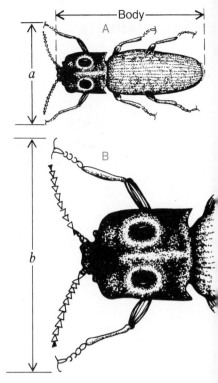

Body A

20.1 (a) Measure the lengths marked *a* and *b* in these two drawings. From the lengths calculate the scale factor of the enlargement from drawing B to 1 d.p.

(b) Measure the length of the beetle's body in drawing A. Calculate the length of the body in the **complete** drawing B. (Only part of B is shown on this page.)

(c) How long would the body be in a 0·6 times reduction of drawing A?

(d) If drawing A is enlarged so that the length marked *a* is enlarged to 3·8 cm, what is the scale factor of the enlargement, to 1 d.p.?

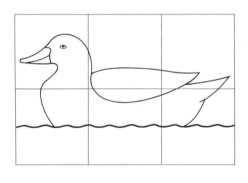

20.2 The squares in this grid are 2 cm by 2 cm.

(a) What size of square would you use to make a 1·2 times enlargement of the drawing?

(b) What size of square would you use to make a 0·8 times reduction of the drawing?

(c) Make a 0·8 times reduction of the drawing, as accurately as you can.

20.3 What is the scale factor of each of these enlargements or reductions?

(a) A to B   (b) B to A   (c) C to A

(d) A to D   (e) D to C   (f) C to D

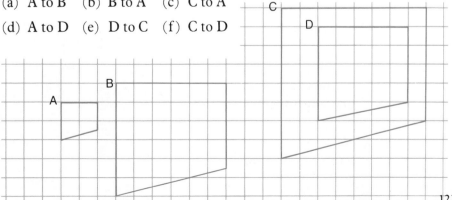

21 Statistics

21.1 Here are the weights in kilograms of the girls and the boys in a fourth-year class.

Girls 47, 61, 50, 50, 60, 55, 52, 54, 52, 50, 48, 53, 57, 54, 61
Boys 43, 59, 47, 59, 65, 62, 62, 58, 53, 70, 55, 57

(a) Draw two scales and mark the weights on them by dots.

(b) Calculate the mean weight of each group and mark its position on the scale.

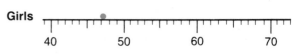

(c) In which group are the weights more widely spread out? Calculate the range for each group.

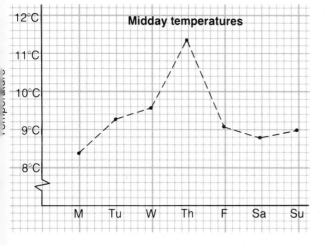

21.2 This graph shows the midday temperatures during one week.

(a) Calculate the mean midday temperature for that week.

(b) Calculate the range of the midday temperatures during that week.

(c) Can you use the graph to find the temperature at midnight between Thursday and Friday? If so, what was the temperature then?

21.3 A survey of people's ages was carried out in a village. The results are shown in this chart.

(a) Calculate the percentage of the total population in each of the five age groups.

(b) What percentage of the village population is aged 60 or over?

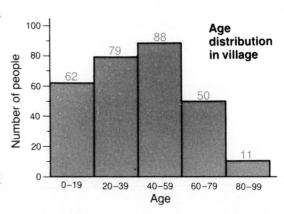

122

21.4 Eight people work in the accounts department of a company.
The manager of the department is paid £260 a week.
The assistant manager gets £220 a week.
The manager's secretary gets £120 a week, and the assistant manager's secretary gets £100.

There are four clerical staff, each of whom gets £90 a week.

One of the clerical staff complains to her trade union that people in the accounts department are poorly paid. The manager tells the union that the average (mean) weekly pay in the department is £132·50.

(a) Show that the manager is right in what he says, by doing the calculation yourself.

(b) Why is the mean weekly pay misleading in this case?

22 Probability

22.1 A youth club has a raffle. There is only one prize – the latest album by one of the best groups around. 200 tickets are sold.

(a) Karen has bought tickets numbered 1, 2, 199 and 200.
Paul has bought numbers 41, 73, 136 and 184.
Does Paul have a better chance of winning than Karen? If so, why?

(b) David has bought tickets 48, 49, 50, 51 and 52.
What is the probability that David will win?

22.2 Anar has a pack of cards, each with a number and a letter on it.

A	A	A	B	B	C	C	C	C	D	D	D
1	2	3	3	4	4	5	6	7	7	8	9

She puts the cards face down on the table, and shuffles them about. Her friend Gary takes a card. What is the probability that

(a) he picks a card with a letter A on it

(b) he picks a card with an even number on it

(c) he picks a card with a number divisible by 3

(d) he picks a card with a number divisible by 4

(e) he picks a card with a letter C and an odd number on it

22.3 The fish in a tank consist of 5 black males, 3 black females, 7 white males and 3 white females. If someone puts their hand in the tank and takes out a fish without looking, what is the probability that

(a) they take out a male fish   (b) they take out a black fish
(c) they take out a female fish   (d) they take out a white fish

23 Arranging and selecting

23.1 Four classes, A, B, C and D, each have practical exams in four subjects: science, woodwork, metalwork and home economics.

The exams all take place in a period of five days, from Monday to Friday.

Each exam lasts a whole day, and has to be done in the proper room. There is only one science room, one woodwork room, one metalwork room and one home economics room. In each room there is only enough space for one class at a time.

No class can have exams on four days running.

The home economics room is not available on Tuesday.

(a) Copy this exam timetable and complete it. Class A's exams are already fixed.

	Mon	Tues	Wed	Th	Fri
A	Sci.		H.E.	Wood.	Met.
B					
C					
D					

(b) Suppose it is Monday, not Tuesday, when the home economics room is not available. See if you can complete the timetable in this case. (All the other rules still apply.)

23.2 A school invites three MPs to give talks at a meeting. They are a Labour MP, a Conservative MP and a Liberal MP.

The organiser of the meeting has to decide who is to speak first, who is to speak second and who third.

How many different possible orders of speaking are there? (For example, 'Conservative, Liberal, Labour' is one possible order.)

23.3 A tennis team consists of Alice, Brenda and Carol (girls), and David, Edward and Fergus (boys).

One boy and one girl have to be chosen to represent the team at a prizegiving. In how many ways can the pair be chosen?

23.4 A club has to choose a chairman and a secretary. There are four people to choose from: A, B, C and D.

What different ways are there to fill the two jobs?

(For example, A could be chairman and B secretary, or B could be chairman and A secretary, and so on.)

M Miscellaneous questions

The questions in this section are taken from the SMP 11-16 pilot 16+ examination
(papers 1 and 2) and are reprinted with the kind permission of the Oxford and
Cambridge Schools Examination Board and the East Anglian Examinations Board.

M1 How much less do you pay if you
buy this stereo player in the sale,
instead of at the normal price?

M2 Rajesh was born in 1969.
In what year will he be 65 years old (assuming he lives that long)?

M3 Write down a number which is between 3·6 and 3·7

M4 Calculate $\frac{3}{4}$ of £6.

M5 Brenda is painting this fence.
It has taken 30 minutes to paint from A to B.

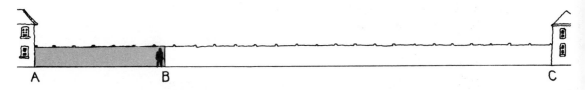

A   B   C

Estimate how long it will take her to paint from B to C,
if she works at the same speed.

M6 Bottle A holds 0·7 litre.

Bottle B holds half as much as bottle A.

How much does bottle B hold?

PANAMA

A handsome range in
mohair effect velvet covers.
Three seater settee and
two easy chairs.
Previous Price £617.00

SALE PRICE £395

M7 The advert shows the previous price and
the sale price of some furniture.

How much do you save by buying
at the sale price?

M8 Give the number of people watching
the match correct to the nearest
hundred.

M9 Diana has to catch a plane to New York.

The plane leaves at 1040.
Diana has to check in at the airport at least $1\frac{1}{2}$ hours before
the plane leaves.

(a) What is the latest time at which she can check in?

(b) The journey from her home to the airport can take anything
from 30 to 40 minutes, depending on the traffic.

What is the latest time Diana can leave home to be **sure** of
getting to the airport on time?

M10 Calculate 16% of £125.

M11 Work out   (a) $5 + (8 - 6)$ (b) $16 \div (8 \div 2)$

M12 Joan was paid £9·00 for 5 hours' work.
Sadia was paid £6·60 for $3\frac{1}{2}$ hours' work

Which girl was paid more per hour?
Show how you decide.

M13 Helen took her baby to the clinic every Friday to be weighed.

Here is part of the baby's weight record.

July 22nd	4·380 kg
July 29th	4·550 kg
	4·700 kg
August 12th	4·910 kg

(a) One of the dates is missing. The doctor forgot to write it in at the time.
What is the missing date?

(b) How much weight did the baby gain between July 22nd and July 29th? Write the answer in **kilograms**.

(c) Change your answer to part (b) into **grams**.

M14 Patsy is putting up a shelf on the wall of her room.

The wall is 350 cm long.

The shelf is 270 cm long.

Patsy wants the spaces at each end of the shelf to be of equal width.

How wide does each of the spaces have to be?

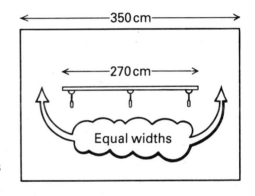

M15 The length of a newspaper headline depends on the letters in it.
For example, small a counts 1 unit, but capital A counts 2 units.

Here is a table showing the numbers of units for each letter, and for spaces between words.

Small letters

i , l	$\frac{1}{2}$
m , w	$1\frac{1}{2}$
all others	1

Capital letters

I	$\frac{1}{2}$
M , W	$2\frac{1}{2}$
all others	2

Spaces between words	2

What is the length, in units, of this headline?

Wales wins

127

M16 (a) Write down the coordinates of the points A, B, C and D.

(b) If the two lines AB and CD are continued upwards, they will meet.

Write down the coordinates of the point where they will meet.

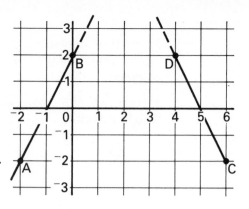

M17

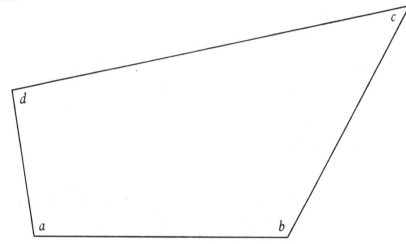

(a) Which is the smallest of the angles *a*, *b*, *c*, *d*?

(b) Which is the largest angle?

M18

Robert is with his mother and father.
Robert is 100 cm tall.
Estimate how tall his mother is.

M19 Here are six numbers: 58·69   58·648   58·069   58·6   58·099   57·9

(a) Which of the numbers is the largest?

(b) Which of the numbers are smaller than 58·5?

M20 Mr and Mrs Jones rent a house for a month.
They agree to pay for the electricity they use.

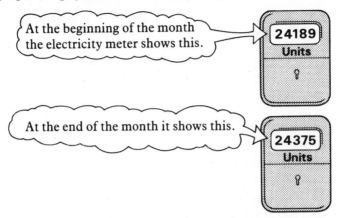

At the beginning of the month the electricity meter shows this. → 24189 Units

At the end of the month it shows this. → 24375 Units

(a) How many units did Mr and Mrs Jones use?

(b) One unit costs them 5p. Calculate the cost of the electricity they used.

M21 A bar of chocolate is 12 cm by 5 cm by 2 cm.

These are drawings of four boxes of different sizes.

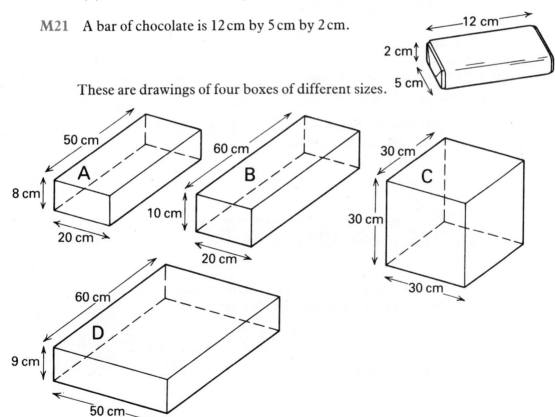

(a) Which one of the boxes A, B, C and D can be filled exactly with whole bars of chocolate?

(b) How many bars can be packed into the box you have chosen?

M22 Malcolm has been asked to put some boxes like the one shown here . . .

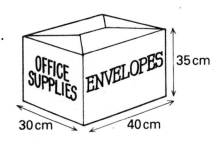

35 cm

30 cm   40 cm

. . . against the wall of a store room which is 450 cm long.

←————— 450 cm —————→

(a) How many boxes can he fit along the wall if he puts them in a line this way round?

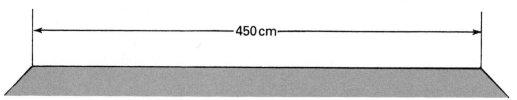

(b) How many boxes can he fit along the wall if he puts them in a line this way round?

M23 A theatre manager kept a record of the number of people watching a play each night the play was on.

	Mon.	Tues.	Wed.	Thurs.	Fri.	Sat.
Number of people	18	24	26	19	226	263

(a) How many people altogether watched the play?

(b) Calculate the mean (average) number of people per night.

(c) Why does this average number give a misleading idea of the number of people watching the play each night?

M24 (a) Copy the diagram on the right.

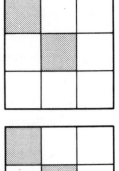

Shade one of the white squares,
so that afterwards the drawing has
just **one** line of reflection symmetry.

Then draw the line of symmetry.

(b) Copy the diagram on the right.

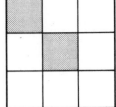

Shade one of the white squares
so that afterwards the drawing has
two lines of reflection symmetry.

Then draw the two lines of symmetry.

M25 The same model of colour TV is on sale in two shops, A and B.

Shop A

Shop B

Calculate the cost of buying the TV before the end of June

(a) from shop A   (b) from shop B

M26 This is a drawing of a model church.

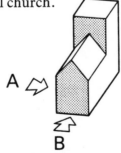

(a) Which of these is the view from A?

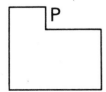

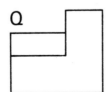

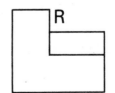

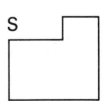

(b) Sketch the view from B.

M27 (a) Martin weighs 10 stone 8 pounds.
1 stone is equal to 14 pounds.

How many pounds does Martin weigh?

(b) Martin has a French friend called Pierre.
Pierre weighs 62 kg.

Use the graph below to find out which of the two boys is heavier.

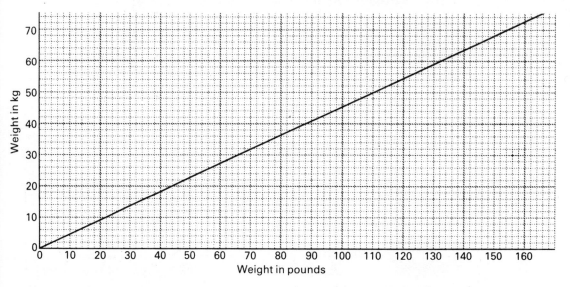

(c) What is the difference in weight between the two boys, in kilograms?

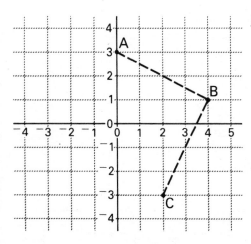

M28 Copy the diagram on the left.

(a) Write down the coordinates of the points A, B and C.

(b) A, B and C are three corners of a square.
The fourth corner is at a point D.
Mark the position of D on the diagram.

(c) Write down the coordinates of D.

M29 Here is a recipe for shortbread biscuits.

> To make 8 shortbread biscuits you need
>
> 100 g plain flour   50 g ground rice
>
> 50 g caster sugar   100 g butter
>
> $\frac{1}{2}$ teaspoon salt

(a) How much flour will you need to make 20 biscuits?

(b) How much caster sugar will you need to make 20 biscuits?

M30 Nurses in hospital make a record of how much fluid a patient takes in each day (his **intake**) and how much he gives out (his **output**).

This graph shows a patient's intake and output of fluid during one week.

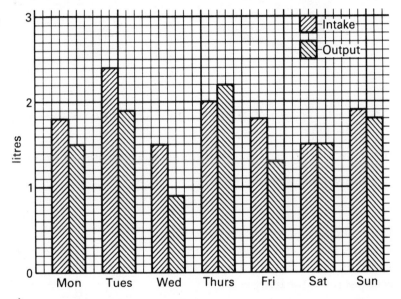

(a) On which day was the patient's output greater than his intake?

(b) What was the patient's intake on Tuesday, in litres?

(c) What was the difference between the intake and the output on Wednesday? Write the answer first in **litres**, then in **millilitres**.

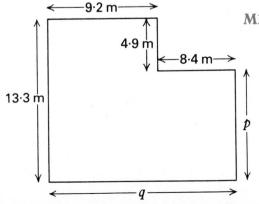

M31 This is the floor plan of a room. The drawing is not to scale. All the corners of the room are right-angles.

(a) Find the missing lengths p and q.

(b) Calculate the perimeter of the room.

(c) Calculate the area of the floor in square metres.

M32 Two shops, A and B, sell coloured paper for children to cut up and make shapes.

Shop A sells a pack of 25 sheets for £1.

Each sheet is 30 cm by 40 cm.

Shop B sells a pack of 20 sheets for £1.

Each sheet is 35 cm by 45 cm.

(a) What is the area, in square centimetres, of **one** of the sheets in pack A?

(b) Which pack, A or B, gives you more paper for your money?

Show your working clearly.

M33 On a school trip, five boys, Alan, Bob, Charlie, David and Edward, plan to travel on the back seat. The back seat has room for five people.

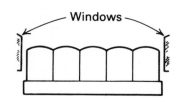

Adam and Bob always sit together.

Charlie and David often fight, so there must be at least two people between them.

Edward cannot sit next to a window because it makes him sick.

Find all the possible arrangements in which the five boys can sit. Use A for Adam, B for Bob, and so on.

M34 Neeta made this design by sticking five coloured circles on to paper.

In which order did she stick the circles down?

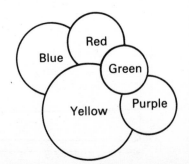

M35 Pupils at Hillside School all study English and Maths in the third year. They have to choose 5 more subjects.

The subjects available are:

Foreign languages: French, German, Spanish

Sciences: Physics, Chemistry, Biology

Others: History, Geography, Art, Nutrition, Craft

Not all combinations of subjects are allowed. To find out if a combination is allowed, you have to go through this flow chart.

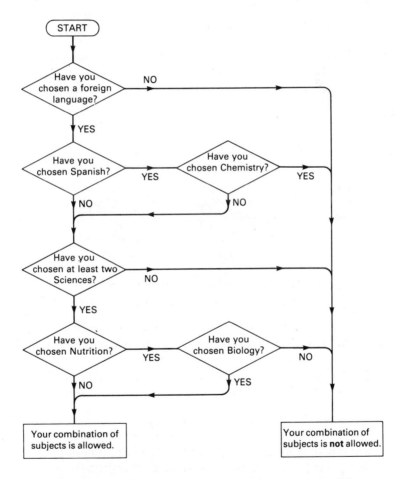

Use the flow chart to find out if these combinations of subjects are allowed or not. Write 'yes' or 'no' for each combination.

(a) French, Chemistry, Spanish, Geography, Physics
(b) Chemistry, Geography, History, Biology, Art
(c) Biology, Nutrition, French, Physics, Geography
(d) German, Art, Biology, Spanish, Nutrition

M36 A sliced loaf is 24 cm long.
Each side is 8 mm thick.

How many slices are there in the loaf?

M37 (a) One way to buy 3 litres of wine
is to buy three 1-litre bottles.
How much would this cost?

(b) Write down another way to buy
3 litres. How much would this cost?

(c) Write down yet another way to buy
3 litres. How much would this cost?

(d) Which is the cheapest way to buy
3 litres?

White Wine
1 litre
£2·49

White Wine
1½ litres
£3·55

White Wine
2 litres
£4·55

M38 Carol has £12·50 to spend on records.
There are four records she would like to buy.

A	B	C	D
£4·30	£3·70	£4·60	£3·80

(a) She cannot afford to buy all four records.
How much **more** money would she need, to buy all four?

(b) She can afford to buy three of the records. (Remember she has £12·50.)
Which three could they be? (There are two answers. Give them both.)

M39 The longest known species of seaweed is the Pacific giant kelp.
It can grow up to 60 metres in length, and can grow 45 centimetres
in a day.

If it is 20 m long now, and grows 45 cm every day, how many days
will it take from now to grow to its full length of 60 m?
Give your answer to the nearest whole number.

M40 These drawings show two tiles of
the same thickness and made from
the same material.

The smaller tile weighs 24 g.

How much does the larger tile weigh?

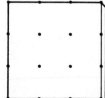

M41 A girl sells soft drinks from a market stall on Saturday.
She has to pay £15 rent for the stall.

She buys cans of soft drink in boxes of 12.
She pays £2·16 for a box of 12 cans.
She sells the cans at 30p each.

(a) What does she pay for each can?

(b) How much profit does she make on each can?

(c) How many cans does she have to sell to make enough money
to pay the rent of the stall?

M42 The diagram shows a lucky spinner.
The spinner has been tested to check
that it is fair.

(a) What is the probability that the
arrow will point to a grey section
when it stops?

(b) What is the probability that it points
to a number greater than 4 when
it stops?

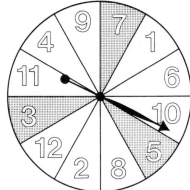

M43 Pam is going to cycle from Penzance to Aberdeen, a distance of 720 miles.
After the first 4 days, she has covered 166 miles.

(a) What was her average number of miles per day during the
first 4 days?

(b) Suppose she continues at the same average rate until she has
completed the journey.
How many days will she take to complete the rest of the journey?
(Part of a day counts as a day.)

M44 A surveyor wishes to find the length of a flagpole
on the top of a high building.
This sketch shows the measurements he makes.

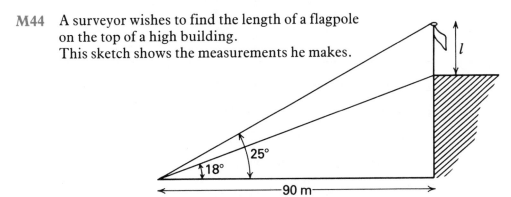

(a) Make an accurate scale drawing. (Write down the scale you use.)

(b) Find the length of the flagpole (marked *l* on the sketch).

M45 The energy value of foods can be
measured in calories.
This table gives the number of
calories in 100 grams of various
foods.

Food	Number of calories in 100 g
White bread	250
Butter	750
Cheese	400

A sandwich is made up of 50 g of white bread, 10 g of butter and
60 g of cheese.

(a) Calculate the number of calories in (i) the bread (ii) the butter (iii) the cheese
(b) Calculate the total number of calories in the sandwich.

M46 Here are two pictures of the sea, taken from above.
Picture B was taken **1 minute later** than picture A.
The dotted line shows the position of one particular wave.

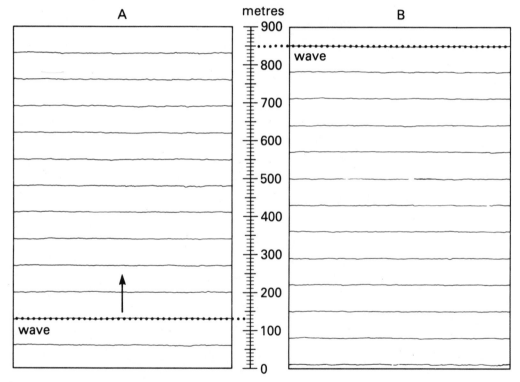

(a) How far did the dotted wave move in 1 minute?

(b) Calculate the speed of the wave in metres per second.

(c) When the sea is fairly shallow, there is a formula for calculating its depth
when you know the speed of the wave. The formula is $d = \dfrac{s^2}{9 \cdot 8}$.

   d stands for the depth in metres.
   s stands for the speed of the waves in metres per second.

   Use this formula to calculate the depth of the sea shown in the picture.

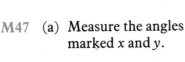
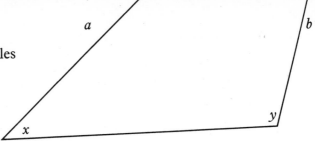

M47 (a) Measure the angles marked x and y.

(b) If the lines a and b are continued, they will meet.
Calculate the angle at the point where they meet.
Show your working.

M48 Sandra goes fruit picking. This is something she has never done before.

At first she picks slowly.
Then she gets better at it until she is able to pick quite quickly.
Then she gets tired and picks more slowly until she stops when the basket is full.

Copy the axes below, and sketch a graph to show how the amount of fruit in Sandra's basket increases as she picks.

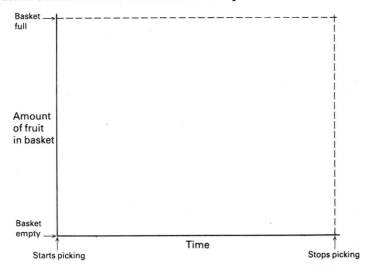

M49 Dress manufacturers use these formulas when they are designing clothes for 'average' women.

$$w = \frac{h}{2} - 20 \qquad s = \frac{w}{2} + 5$$

h stands for the woman's height, in cm.
w stands for the waist measurement, in cm.
s stands for the shoulder measurement, in cm.

(a) What would be the waist measurement of a woman 170 cm tall?

(b) Calculate the waist and shoulder measurements of a woman who is 164 cm tall.

(c) Calculate the waist measurement of a woman whose shoulder measurement is 45 cm.

139

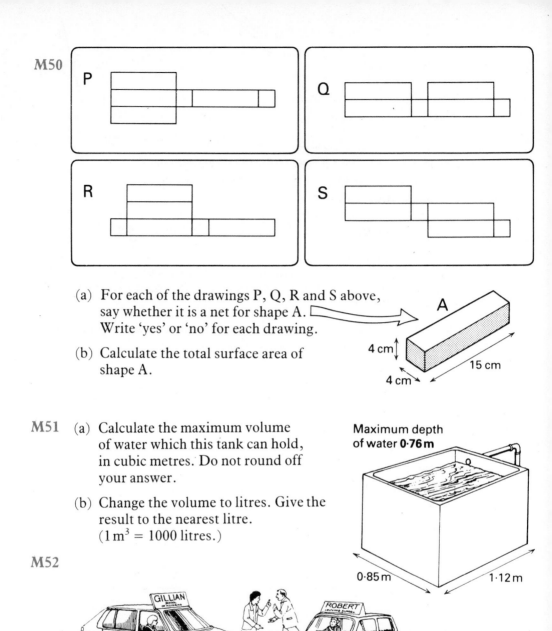

M50

(a) For each of the drawings P, Q, R and S above, say whether it is a net for shape A. Write 'yes' or 'no' for each drawing.

(b) Calculate the total surface area of shape A.

M51 (a) Calculate the maximum volume of water which this tank can hold, in cubic metres. Do not round off your answer.

(b) Change the volume to litres. Give the result to the nearest litre. ($1\,m^3 = 1000$ litres.)

M52

Gillian and Robert each run a driving school.

During the last 12 months, 317 of Gillian's learner drivers took their driving test for the first time. 132 of them passed.

During the same period, 422 of Robert's learner drivers took their test for the first time. 189 of them passed.

Which driving school has the better record of first-time passes? **Show clearly how you get your answer.**